DEAF SCHOOL

The Non-Stop Pop Art Punk Rock Party

DEAF SCHOOL

The
Non-Stop Pop Art
Punk Rock Party

Paul Du Noyer
With a foreword by Suggs

Liverpool University Press

First published 2013 by
Liverpool University Press
4 Cambridge Street
Liverpool
L69 7ZU

British Library Cataloguing-in-Publication data
A British Library CIP record is available

ISBN 978-1-84631-860-3 limp

Typeset by Carnegie Book Production, Lancaster
Printed and bound by Short Run Press Ltd, Exeter

Contents

Foreword

Suggs

B ACK IN MY YOUTH I met some characters who were a right bunch, but what we had in common was that we loved Deaf School. It's strange how this theatrical band from Liverpool touched the children of North London.

In Madness we'd all listened to Deaf School records. Their first album was a big phenomenon in our lives. In 1975 they played at the Roundhouse in Camden, which was the greatest music venue in the world as far as we were concerned, and I was bowled over by them. You'd had glam rock, which was starting to go all brickies in stack-heel boots. Even pub rock was getting flabby. But Deaf School seemed to elevate themselves above everything. Though they occasionally played in pubs, you were transported into some faded theatre at the turn of the century.

They totally informed the way we formed Madness. It was inspiring that you could have that many people on stage. They offered you the whole mixture, the all-encompassing night out. The music itself was absorbing, but with the visual theatricality you really had 180 degrees. The interaction of different people on stage, the fact that we had saxophone, piano, two vocalists – a lot of things came from Deaf School. And we loved the notion that they all had pseudonyms, like Enrico Cadillac. This was all before punk, when everyone did it. Or Max Ripple, stopping the show half way through to deliver a sermon on the dangers of celery. Bette Bright, though, was the one that caught my eye...

Our band was an unruly bunch of yobbos, but we liked fashion and we liked music. We got our first gig at the Hope & Anchor in Islington, a proper music pub and a big deal for us. We knew the guv'nor, because we'd been hanging around there and used to put Deaf School songs on the jukebox. The place only held about 40 people, but we heard that Deaf School were in town – and they were coming to see us!

So I remember backstage after the gig, which was the gentlemen's toilets. I was strolling in the direction of the delightful Miss Bright, just in time to overhear her saying, 'I thought the band were great. But the singer's not *all that*.' Which was my first engagement with the delightful Miss Bright. Well, I may not have had it all, but I had enough to get her to come out with me.

What an amazing time. I was 18 years old, I was in a band and I was going out with a pretty spectacular pop star, in the shape of Bette Bright. We have now been married for more than thirty years.

Next thing we were rehearsing in the basement of a dentist's surgery in Finchley Road, among a collection of plaster casts of North London gnashers. Deaf School's leader Clive Langer came along to see about producing us, and the rest is history. Just like Deaf School, we distrusted everyone. We had our own insulated community of 15 or 20 kids, all into retro gear and doing our own thing. And Clive just seemed to understand what we were doing, because of what he'd wanted from Deaf School. We clicked straight away and he produced all our hits.

The question is, why didn't Deaf School make it? Nobody knows. It's one of the greatest mysteries in pop. The obvious thing was that punk came along and washed them away. Madness were lucky because we were on the tail end of Deaf School, and we picked up their baton. We weren't as theatrical, but what they laid down informed what we were about to do – with videos, with dressing up, playing characters. Being a bit less serious without being stupid. By 1978 it was all new wave, and you could be glamorous again, foolish without being fools. It was possible to have a good time.

For me, the gigs Deaf School have done recently have been some of the best I've seen by *any* band. It's not just nostalgia. One of the first times I got on stage with them, I'd had a few cold drinks and I was a bit emotional. I was going to join in 'What a Way to End it All', and I said, 'I've got to tell you: Deaf School were one of the biggest influences on Madness.' And some Scouse wag shouted, 'Where the fuck did it all go wrong then?' Which slightly put me off my stride.

That being said, it delights me to know that their full story is finally being told. Please enjoy…

Acknowledgements

THE ABUNDANT HELP I received in writing this book is proof of Deaf School's place in many hearts. But my thanks go firstly to all the current band members, who gave unstintingly of their time: Steve Allen (alias Enrico Cadillac Jnr), Clive Langer, Steve Lindsey (Mr Average), Anne Martin (Bette Bright), Ian Ritchie and John Wood (the Revd Max Ripple). Equally generous was their indefatigable mentor/facilitator Ken Testi.

My other main interviewees were Doreen Allen, Phil Allen, Nicky Allt, Neville Astley, Hazel Bartram-Birchenough, Bryan Biggs, Will Birch, Joan Bonenfant, Bernie Connor, Rob Dickins, Geoff Davies, Mike Evans, Colin Fallows, Peter Halligan, Steve Hardstaff, Sandra Harris (alias Sandy Bright), Norman Killon, Paul Pilnick, Dave Sargeant, David Saunders, Laurence Sidorczuk, Frank Silver, Suggs, Kevin Ward and Dave Wibberley. My thanks to all.

I should also mention the late Derek Taylor, a mentor for the band and an inspiration to me. When I interviewed him for *Q* magazine in 1988 we used about 30 minutes of spare cassette tape discussing our mutual obsession with Deaf School. Parts of that conversation have already appeared in my book *Liverpool: Wondrous Place*, but I felt it worth reprising them here.

Special thanks to Kevin McManus for allowing me to use his 1994 interview with Sam Davis (alias Eric Shark).

For their kind help with my research: Nigel Blackwell, Jayne Casey, Marilyn Castleton, Alan Clayson, Sara Cohen, Mark Davies Markham, Paul Gallagher, Philip Hayes, Lesley Kazan-Pinfield, David Lloyd, Fiona Looney, Ian McNabb, Joe Musker, Henry Priestman, Angie Sammons, Spizz and Judy Totton.

At least as important as anyone else I've mentioned is Mark Adamson, supremo of the band's superb website *Deafschoolmusic.com*. Mark shared his knowledge generously and organised more than one unforgettable night out along the way. I have him to thank for this book's Discography, and I relied heavily on the All Time Gig List he is compiling on the site. Via *Deafschoolmusic* and elsewhere, I have been contacted by numerous Deaf School fans with wonderful memories to share. Special thanks to Tony Zaidel.

Final nods of sincere gratitude go to my wife Una Du Noyer, my agent Ros Edwards at Edwards Fuglewicz, and my editor Anthony Cond at Liverpool University Press.

Introduction

FORTY YEARS AGO A chaotic student group played their debut show, at the Liverpool art school Christmas dance. They were called Deaf School because they rehearsed in a former school for the deaf. It was a throwaway name for a pop-up band, who took defiant pride in being below-average musicians. And yet, somehow, they seemed to do something right.

Word spread, their audiences grew. Record companies came sniffing. Large cheques were produced and champagne corks popped. Twelve years earlier the Liverpool music scene had given the world the Beatles. Could lightning strike twice in the same place? A lot of entirely sane people agreed that this band could be the future of British rock'n'roll.

They weren't, of course. Chart success eluded Deaf School, for reasons that are still being thrashed out in pubs around the country. Most of all their timing was unlucky.

They played a brash, splashy, infectious sort of rock cabaret, just as punk rock was about to explode. ('They were a great band,' said the Sex Pistols' manager Malcolm McLaren, 'but it's just as bad being too early as too late.') Deaf School broke up in 1978, somewhat disillusioned. Eventually, though, after varied and often spectacular solo careers, its members reunited and played to joyful audiences. Some very major pop stars acclaimed them as an influence.

That's why I start from the premise that Deaf School are an artistic success and not a commercial failure. Posterity has its own hit parade and I think Deaf School will be high in it. It's a measure of this band's strange, anomalous position in British pop that their story connects such disparate names as Queen and Elvis Costello. They don't sit along any neat continuum. In fact they inhabited a fracture-line between two eras, and they nearly slipped right down it, forever.

Deaf School were pop art, they were their own mad kind of punk rock, and they were always a guaranteed non-stop party. They should have been big, but that doesn't matter now. They are something to celebrate and to cherish. Deaf School are such a delicious secret, it's almost a shame to share it.

The core of this book is my interviews with all surviving members of the band. One challenge in writing their story is their habit of switching, even in mid-sentence, between their stage and civilian names. By and large I'll refer to them by their Deaf School identities but the occasional parentheses will be needed for clarity. So let me introduce the six key characters.

Clive Langer, sometimes known as Cliff Hanger, is the group's lead guitarist and musical director. Bespectacled and watchful on the stage, he looks like a man who is cautious of lunatics taking over his asylum. After Deaf School he became one of the world's foremost record producers, working with Madness, Elvis Costello (with whom he co-wrote the classic song 'Shipbuilding'), Dexys Midnight Runners, David Bowie and many others.

Enrico Cadillac Jnr, or plain Steve Allen, is the lead male vocalist. His Deaf School persona suggests Clark Gable, or a sleazy private eye, or a Latin American gigolo, or a Scouse lounge lizard. He went on to form more bands, find solo stardom in Europe and have a glittering career in A&R.

Bette Bright, alias Anne Martin, is the female vocalist and last remaining member of the Bright Sisters, who were a much-appreciated element in Deaf School's early line-up. She too enjoyed a rewarding solo career and is married to one of Deaf School's earliest fans, Suggs of Madness.

Mr Average, sometimes Frankie Average but always Steve Lindsey, is the ostentatiously unassuming bass-player. After Deaf School's first career he hung up his imitation Beatle suit to form the Planets and then moved into music publishing.

The Revd Max Ripple, otherwise known as John Wood, is the keyboard player with a warped ecclesiastical manner. Max/John was a tutor at Liverpool art college when most of the band were students and has since gone on to be Emeritus Professor of Design at Goldsmiths College.

Ian Ritchie, the saxophonist, is always known as Ian Ritchie, which will simplify our task a little. Still a hard-working career musician, he's been a prolific composer, producer and a regular in the bands of superstars like Roger Waters.

In a saga as long as Deaf School's, in a line-up that was seldom fixed for very long, there are plenty of other musicians who have passed through the ranks and we shall meet most of them. But special mention must be made of the singer Sam Davis (known onstage as Eric Shark) and the drummer Tim Whittaker, each of whom has sadly passed on. I hope they will not be overlooked in what follows.

ONE

Tramcar to Frankenstein

*The Surrealist Republic of Liverpool 8 – Clive Admires
Enrico's Trousers – A New Noise in the Deaf School*

H IGH ON A CITY HILL is the Anglican Cathedral of
Liverpool, in brown square-shouldered loneliness like
a double-crossed gothic gangster, wondering where its
world went. Climb to the top of that tall tower and look
down. See all the little dramas of love and lust, riot and
poverty, played out by those tiny figures in the streets,
chasing their insect destinies.

Up here we can see for miles. Buffeted by winds from
the Irish Sea we try to make sense of Liverpool. Well,
we try. What are those? Giant steel turbines rotate idly
out west in Liverpool Bay. Grey distance, Ireland behind.
Beyond that, next stop Pier 92, West 52nd Street. On the
skyline a vast spread of bruised blue Welsh mountains. But

nearer, two silver strips of river, the Dee and the Mersey, defining that weird peninsula the Wirral, mystically known as 'across the water'. We see pony-owning villages and dying publand proletowns.

Back over here, at the water's edge two Liver birds perch above a tangle of city streets built for warehouses and whorehouses and counting houses, and everything needful for an enormous seaport. Docks are difficult, nature-defying beasts and they were invented here. In fact the modern Mersey manhandles more cargo then ever, only it's no longer men who handle it, just cranes and tin boxes. But there are those Panama-busting ships out in the squally estuary with their midget escorts the pilots and the tugs. Curving in their wake are little white ferries to Birkenhead, and bigger ones to Dublin and the Isle of Man.

Turning to look inland we see some vaguely green horizon. Travellers from this eastern region speak of a land called Lancashire. They describe the mighty city of Manchester. Perhaps they are right. Liverpudlians are not so sure.

Whatever. The River Mersey we'll file away in our minds, and those downtown streets we'll soon revisit. Now, look down below. Right down at Gambier Terrace, regal as a queen and full of secrets. At her feet, the vertiginous cliff-face of St James's Cemetery, a mossy necropolis in the void of a former quarry, dug in the sandstone spine that separates Liverpool from England. North along that spinal ridge sits Hope Street. From Gambier Terrace it passes the former School of Art, the two Philharmonics (Hall and pub) and the Everyman Theatre, ending at the retro space-age Catholic Cathedral. The art school's successor is down there as well.

A lot of our story happened along Hope Street and the majestic streets around it – Catharine, Canning, Huskisson – or on the broad descent of Hardman Street which slouches down into town. Here, in fact, is the much-mythologised district of Liverpool 8 (though some of its landmarks are technically outside that district). The name is more than merely a postal zone. If Liverpool is not exactly England, then Liverpool 8 is not exactly Liverpool. In the city's psychic geography it came to represent two worlds outside the Scouse mainstream, worlds we can roughly summarise as 'foreigners' and 'white layabouts'. If you'd grown up locally with any inclination to *la vie bohème* then you were steadily drawn here on both accounts. It offered difference, a thrill of the unfamiliar and perhaps a slight dash of danger.

Its nineteenth-century mansions were built uphill with views of the Mersey's maritime traffic. Ships' owners could lift a telescope and from a parlour window watch their payloads' progress. There also came many humbler people whose living had been from the sea, or who were refugees or would-be emigrants who got no further. And in time they took the bigger houses, too, when the gentry slipped away to leafier retreats and multiple doorbells started appearing beneath the cracked fanlights. The legacy of those days is a multi-cultural principality unto itself, grouped around the great Liverpool 8 highway of Upper Parliament Street.

At the same time, these higher acres were far enough from sordid commerce to be a haven for culture and learning. The university arose and other institutions, including a fine Philharmonic Hall. Broad cobblestoned streets offered magnificent prospects. The better-preserved parts, beloved of film location scouts, are nowadays called the Georgian Quarter. Next to them, red-bricked boulevards lead to noble Victorian parks. Most of what we see has reverted to its medieval name of Toxteth, linked for many with images of ghetto firestorms.

Handsome old precincts still give Liverpool 8 the look of a slightly battered Bloomsbury, and it was often compared to that area, especially when the stolid merchants made way for raffish intellectuals. The look was also reminiscent of Dublin, compounded by the various corner pubs whose tobacco-browned rooms might host the repartee of literary wits or the mournful bellowing of a sentimental drunk. These are important places, these pubs: Ye Cracke, off Hope Street, the Oxford, the Caledonia and the Blackburne, the little Belvedere, the Grapes (alias Peter Kavanagh's) and the opulent 'Phil' itself. Many of the big decisions in our story were taken within their walls. Happily we can still see these pubs from our perch. And occasionally hear them too.

As rents fell, artists and poets found the area congenial and joined the ethnic communities who had made this singular *arrondissement* their own. Dubious late-night joints attracted curious adventurers. And slowly a Kingdom of Outsiders took form here. In the 1950s two students, John Lennon at the art college and Paul McCartney at the grammar school next door, each sensed something wonderfully exotic on their doorstep and hurled themselves at it.

Writers always loved Liverpool 8. They liked the abundance of raw material – professorial flotsam, red-light jetsam – and the contrast of prosperous façades with shadowy backways, and ruined stables whose last horses bolted a hundred years ago. Adrian Henri imagined a wounded young Polish gunman, bleeding in Little St Bride Street. Sean Hignett's story *A Picture to Hang on the Wall* has the kitchen sink anti-glamour of 1960s bring-a-bottle parties, where everyone asks if Roger McGough is here yet. Brian Patten hosted Allen Ginsberg in Canning Street.

John Cornelius prowled the drinking dens to sketch their inhabitants and wrote about them later. Beryl Bainbridge constantly re-lived her local upbringing, weaving in the legend of Adolf Hitler's lost years in Stanhope Street. Her friend, fellow novelist and Liverpool art school drop-out Alice Thomas Ellis wrote of passing an alley and hearing a frightened girl's voice: 'Let me go and you can have yer pound back!' That is the bleakest *haiku* of Liverpool 8.

Deaf School grew from the fertile soil of Liverpool art college. This unique provincial scene was caught between the worlds of artistic academia, cosmopolitan diversity and tough, unpretentious Scouseland. With a pungent identity of its own, Liverpool 8 would draw these dozen young people from all corners of Britain and propel them into reckless, life-changing decisions.

***

We saw from our Cathedral eyrie that Liverpool art college was in the tower's shadow. Its classical façade, 86 Hope Street, dates from 1910. An older part, on Mount Street, has tall studio windows to catch the pale northern light that painters prefer. And on the Upper Duke Street side is a stark post-war extension. Often now you will see a tourist taxi parked nearby, with a Beatle guide to explain why this is hallowed ground. Between 1957 and

1960 the college was home to John Lennon and his friend and fellow Beatle Stuart Sutcliffe.

Adjacent, downhill, is the Liverpool Institute for Performing Arts, or LIPA; formerly the Mechanics Institute, it became a well-regarded grammar school. Paul McCartney was a pupil at Liverpool Institute (as it was then known) from 1953 to 1960, with George Harrison a year behind him. McCartney was later instrumental in founding LIPA in his old school building, while the art college was subsumed into Liverpool John Moores University. By a rich irony, in 2012 Paul's new LIPA expanded into John's old college, thus saving it from redevelopment into flats.

Lennon lived for a time across Hope Street in beatnik squalor at 3 Gambier Terrace. When he married Cynthia, a fellow art student, they borrowed Brian Epstein's flat around the corner in Falkner Street. Like college staff and students of all periods, from Augustus John to Deaf School, they knew the splendid Philharmonic pub, aptly built by the same brewery that founded the city's Walker Art Gallery. Oil-paint and beer mix well in Liverpool 8.

Lennon knew the Cracke, as well, and drank here with friends including Bill Harry and Stuart Sutcliffe, who formed an informal clique called the Dissenters (commemorated by a plaque inside the pub today). They dreamed of giving grimy Liverpool a global reputation through their music, words and painting. Those are the art school dreams that generally vanish when a barmaid shouts Last Orders. But Bill would found a newspaper called *Mersey Beat*, while John and Stuart joined with Paul and George, played rock'n'roll in Hamburg and met local artists like Klaus Voormann and Astrid Kirchherr who helped invent a youth aesthetic that changed the Western world.

The young Beatles rehearsed in the art school canteen, downstairs. The same room was used by their contemporary, Mal Dean, to illustrate the 1970 LP by Piblokto!, a band led by beat poet and Cream lyricist Pete Brown. It was prophetically entitled *Things May Come and Things May Go but the Art School Dance Goes on Forever*. The cross-fertilisation of art, music, drama and poetry became a defining feature of Liverpool 8 in the 1960s. At the far end of Hope Street was Hope Hall, a religious meeting place turned cinema, with a basement venue hosting beatnik arts festivals and proto-hippy 'happenings'. By 1964 Hope Hall was the Everyman Theatre, a radical incubator for gifted young writers and actors. Its basement became the Bistro and more than ever a magnet for scene-makers in search of performance, company and drink.

Out of this milieu would emerge one chart-topping act Scaffold, comprised of John Gorman, Mike McGear (so-named to veil his own identity as Paul McCartney's younger brother) and the poet Roger McGough. The latter, with his friends Brian Patten and Adrian Henri, formed a best-selling triumvirate known as the Mersey Poets. And the protean Henri, teaching at the art college, became an acclaimed painter and the frontman of an avant-garde rock band called the Liverpool Scene. Like Brian Patten, he put up Allen Ginsberg on a 1965 visit that inspired the Beatle-besotted American to pronounce that 'Liverpool is, at the present moment, the centre of consciousness of the human universe.'

Like Sutcliffe (who left the Beatles and stayed in Hamburg, where he was taught by Pop artist Eduardo

Paolozzi), Henri embodied the fusion of musical and visual energy that informed so much creativity in the 1960s. In Liverpool he was part of a charismatic faculty that included the painters Sam Walsh and Maurice Cockrill. Henri staged events at both Hope Hall and the Cavern, straddling uptown art and downtown entertainment. His prodigiously talented band the Liverpool Scene soundtracked the dour Mersey autumn which had followed the Summer of Love, in visionary freak-outs like 'The Entry of Christ into Liverpool' or fractured fantasias like 'Tramcar to Frankenstein'.

∗∗∗

In autumn 1973 the new academic year brought to Liverpool a London boy named Clive Langer. He was already, in some ways, a typical product of the art school/ pop music interface. Born on 19 June 1954, he'd taken his one-year foundation course at Canterbury, attracted there by the town's musical reputation for brainy, jazz-inflected rock acts such as Caravan and Soft Machine. The latter band featured a particular hero of his, the drummer and vocalist Robert Wyatt.

Canterbury's art college was also home to a tutor named Ian Dury, destined for pop stardom with the Blockheads despite his relatively advanced age and the pronounced limp he'd acquired through childhood polio.

'I remember I opened the door for him in a corridor once,' says Clive, 'and he was pissed off, because he was hobbling about and it was as though I was taking the piss out of him. But I was just trying to be gracious.' Dury's band of that time, Kilburn & the High Roads, were frequent Canterbury visitors and their musical style, eclectic, rough-edged, theatrically presented by a sprawling line-up who dressed in artfully improvised jumble-sale clothes, would make a deep impression on the teenage Langer.

After Canterbury he enrolled at Liverpool, largely unaware of the Liverpool 8 scene but certainly conscious of the Lennon connection. 'I chose my art colleges because of the bands that were there. I wasn't that interested in art, I was more interested in music. Lennon was my favourite as a kid. I was in the cloakroom of my primary school, singing "Twist and Shout", screaming my head off in front of my mates. In fact if I'd known about the Dissenters I think I would have called Deaf School the Dissenters. It would have been a good name.'

Growing up in North London his young neighbours included future members of Madness. As early as primary school he played in a Saturday morning band at the Swiss Cottage Odeon. Then, at his grammar school, William Ellis in Highgate, he was inspired by Jethro Tull's Ian Anderson to study the flute: 'I failed my Grade 3, which is the first one you can take. I wanted to play blues flute. I didn't want to learn music. I'm not good at reading music. But I'm smart enough to listen, and to know what I want.' Soon he was in a new band, with his schoolmate, the future film-maker Julien Temple.

'Basically,' Clive explains, 'I'd just been obsessed by bands since I first heard the Shadows. Because of this obsession, I just knew I could get into gigs, it didn't matter if I didn't have a ticket, or I was too young, there were ways. We could bunk into anything. I'd go to loads by helping the band, like at Klook's Kleek [a club at the

Railway Hotel, West Hampstead]: Family, John Mayall. Led Zeppelin I saw on their first tour when they just did some pubs. Like a blues band on speed, quite punky, but later they got a bit grandiose for me.'

With Julien Temple, he went to a Wembley TV studio for the filming of the Rolling Stones' *Rock and Roll Circus*. 'We'd just hear that something was happening and we'd go for it. By the time I was in the sixth form, because of this band I was in with Julien, it opened my ears to John Coltrane, and Weather Report and the Mahavishnu Orchestra. Rock and jazz were mixed up for me after Miles Davis's performance at the Isle of Wight. In fact I was there, and saw Hendrix too.'

Langer's cool determination could well be inherited from his father, a Polish Jew who, alone of his family, escaped the Nazis and settled in London via spells with the British army and the Polish air force. He married an East End girl, became a businessman and in time acquired a couple of hotels in Bloomsbury, the Gresham and the Crichton, which would often serve as Deaf School's base in the capital.

Deaf School's inception can probably be dated to the art school's first day of term in 1973, when Clive Langer noticed another new student who might make a potential ally. 'I thought, Well, *he* looks interesting, he's the only bloke here with slicked-back hair and tight jeans. Everybody else is boring.'

***

The young man who caught Clive's eye was Steve Allen, the future Enrico Cadillac Jnr. Exactly the same thing had happened there sixteen years earlier, when Bill Harry spotted John Lennon, teddy boy rebel among the academic dowdies.

Steve/Enrico takes up the tale: 'On the first day at art college, Clive liked the way I looked, clocked me a bit for clothes, turned-up drainpipe jeans, black Converse, little leather jacket, faint quiff. So he came over to me and asked, "D'you know anywhere good to eat?" I said, If you want really cheap eats, we could go round to the catering college. Whatever they cooked that day was on the menu.'

Langer and Allen found they shared more than a limited food budget and a distaste for flared jeans. 'When I turned up in Liverpool,' Clive says, 'Steve was into the Bowie/Roxy thing, and though I loved the Kinks I was a bit wary of glam. But then I embraced it, and that was the meeting point of musical influences with me and him.' Later they bonded, over bottled beers, on a college coach trip to Blackpool.

An Everton supporter and the only Scouser in Deaf School, Steve Allen spent his early childhood in 66 Huskisson Street, by the Cathedral. He has a memory of feeling afraid when he peered through the railings at the end of his road, down into the deep gorge of St James's Cemetery. With his younger brother, Phil, he later moved to the Old Swan district of the city.

After Steve's parents separated, his father Archie Allen took a flat above a shop by the art college: 'On the corner of Hope Street,' recalls his son, 'over from Gambier Terrace gates. A magic spot. What a view he had of the Cathedral … and all those female fashion students going by!' The apple does not fall far from the tree.

Mr Allen was in fact a large influence on both his

sons. A professional entertainer, he had a one-man act called the Archie Allen Show. He took off Sammy Davis Jr's Las Vegas routine and crooned in the styles of Mel Tormé, Tony Newley and Robert Goulet. He did movie star impressions, from Bogart and Cagney to the more challenging Burt Lancaster. In his wardrobe he kept a tricorn hat, much loved by Steve, for a turn as Marlon Brando's Fletcher Christian.

Steve and Phil's school, Highfield, had a good art department which encouraged the elder brother to take his foundation (or 'pre-Dip') course in Warrington, as a preparation for Liverpool art college.

> The art college is very important in this story because that was a beacon of light for me. I wasn't aware that John Lennon was part of that. It was just a place you'd hang around, and of course it had all those fab girls in the fashion department. But without Liverpool art college and the Cracke around the corner it was pretty dead. Mathew Street was dead.

Today reborn as a hub of Beatles tourism and stag-night mayhem, Mathew Street languished in 1973; in its post-Merseybeat trough the Cavern struggled on a diet of live rock and disco. The Everyman scene, uptown, was a touch too grown-up for the callow Allen, but his passion was nevertheless for poetry.

In 1973 the young versifier was himself published, in Harold and Sylvia Hikins' anthology *Roll the Union On*. And two sights stick with him: a girl in a see-through dress, but no underwear, who watched him give an adolescent reading at Spellow Lane Library; and the monumental Adrian Henri, performing at the Pen & Wig in Harrington Street:

> That was my other beacon of light, seeing Adrian Henri. That was like seeing Allen Ginsberg. Him walking into this small space, cos he was a big character, a big guy, that was exciting. *The Mersey Poets*, in Penguin, that was my main thing. That and seeing whoever Roger Eagle put on at the Stadium. I didn't know any other creative destinations to go to. Liverpool at that time was in danger of becoming like Kendal as far as music goes. Or Warrington. All hairy, every band you saw, heavy rock. That's what Liverpool was.

Roger Eagle, whom he mentions, had arrived in Liverpool to promote local bands at a run-down boxing hall, the Liverpool Stadium. The same venue would soon host a Roxy Music gig, enabling a new tribe of music fans to gather and sense their own community. 'I got a job in W.H. Smith in Penny Lane, Allerton Road,' Steve says, 'and I had to run the record department.

> This was before I went to pre-Dip at Warrington, I had a year off and worked. So the rep came in from Island, and he had [the first Roxy single] 'Virginia Plain'. He said, 'I don't know if you'll get this, mate, a new band, it's a bit off-the-wall.' He put it on and I was like, Oh my God, what the hell is that? It sounds like a rock band with Noel Coward singing! And next thing they came to the Stadium. I ordered that and we sold a lot of them. All the northern cities fell in love with the glamour of Roxy Music and Bowie. Without Roxy where do ABC and the

Human League come from? They all loved Roxy Music. That's why they all loved Deaf School when we came along.

Before Langer and Allen began their songwriting partnership, Steve was writing lyrics. He'd loved so many of his dad's 78 rpm records, including the music hall knockabouts of Flanagan and Allen and Leslie Sarony's 'Ain't it Grand to be Blooming Well Dead'. They were all story songs, and the taste for narrative has never left him. In that vein he wrote and recited 'Cocktails at 8', the comical tale of a thwarted ladies' man. To be submitted as course work, Allen's performance was filmed in the same upstairs room of the Phil where his dad occasionally performed. 'They had the lovely cocktail bar up there, brutally ripped out by some fucking luddite brewery. It was the words *sans* Clive's music at that stage. And the Head of Sculpture played piano in the background for me. What a fabulous place that art school was. Wow!'

∗∗∗

It's significant that 'Cocktails at 8' was course work. Clive and Steve created a pop band, called Deaf School, but Deaf School was also an art project. In that sense it was a true child of the 1960s, when British music was rife with art school alumni. Some, like Ian Dury and Adrian Henri, even combined performance with teaching. There was an earlier tradition of student bands, often with trad jazz roots and a taste for anarchic comedy, like the Alberts, the Temperance Seven and Vivian Stanshall's Bonzo Dog Doo-Dah Band (whose 'doo-dah' came from Dada). But with the post-Beatle flowering of domestic pop, musicians with an art education were suddenly ten-a-penny.

After Liverpool's John Lennon came, among many others, Keith Richards, Charlie Watts and Ronnie Wood of the Rolling Stones; Pete Townshend of the Who and Ray Davies of the Kinks; Eric Clapton, Jimmy Page, Syd Barrett, John Mayall, Cat Stevens, Eric Burdon and Freddie Mercury. Roxy Music's Bryan Ferry and Brian Eno were art school rockers *par excellence.* Punk rock, despite its prole pretensions, was equally connected: examples include Malcolm McLaren, Glen Matlock, Adam Ant, Viv Albertine and most of the Clash. Soon afterwards came Sade, Marc Almond, Jerry Dammers and Clive Langer's friend Mike Barson of Madness.

Entry to art schools became harder than it was in Lennon's day, when a bright but wayward 17-year-old could take the National Diploma in Design. A year after John left Liverpool there was a new Diploma in Art & Design (DipAD), requiring five GCEs and a one-year foundation (or pre-Dip) course. By the time Deaf School left college the standard course led to a BA degree, and art departments have increasingly been pulled into the formal structures of higher education. (Liverpool's art school had already joined the city's polytechnic, and would later be part of Liverpool John Moores University.) In 1973, though, art colleges were still a wonderfully indulgent boot camp for future musicians.

As places where inquisitive young people might gather, conspire, experiment and theorise – and with at least a modest grant to support them – art colleges could host both feckless dreamers and disciplined practitioners. Enjoying a temporary haven from the adult world of work (or lack of it) the art student had a three-year window of self-discovery. Throw in the fringe benefits of access to rehearsal space, print facilities and fashion expertise, plus a few *simpatico* tutors, and rich possibilities arose. Deaf School's members did not waste the opportunity.

'By the end of that first term,' says Clive, 'we'd got this idea we could start a band.

> It came from my obsession, and I realised Steve was into poetry and it might fit. And his dad was a singer and he could sing, so that was how it all started. It was quite conceptual: the idea that we'd ever make a record was totally alien, it was really just, Let's do this thing! It was fun and there was a social side to it, and we couldn't have done it without the art college because we used their PA and the Deaf School and other rooms to practise in.

It should be explained that 'the Deaf School' was an annexe of the college's Fine Art department, situated about half a mile away at the top of Oxford Street (where John Lennon was born). A dignified nineteenth-century building, Crown Street School for the Deaf had served its original purpose until 1948, and was partly demolished before acquisition by the art school. A friend and tutor of the band, Steve Hardstaff, recalls the rest as being ramshackle and cold in winter. Another student, Bryan Biggs, remembers one studio being in a former children's bathroom. At the edge of the university district, where academia makes way for rough-and-tumble Liverpool, the School for the Deaf has since been completely demolished and replaced with modern flats.

Before the Deaf School, though, the embryonic group

spent time at that legendary basement of 86 Hope Street, practising in the same canteen used by the Beatles. Clive:

> We started off rehearsing in the main college, downstairs, then we moved because we were making so much noise. We had that space, and it meant we could rehearse at least once a week. But it was very hard work getting people together and organising it and shouting and screaming at people to shut up and do it. I became the organiser, because I *was*, I suppose. I started it with Steve but really it was me who really wanted to start a band and I talked him into it, and he quite liked it.

Entirely without a musical map, the first rehearsals involved anyone with any type of instrument, or party piece or inclination to show off. A troupe of girl singers came together. Clive surveyed the chaos, and pondered, Steve turned up to sing, and sometimes he didn't turn up at all.

As mentioned, among Clive's influences were the Canterbury-connected Kilburn & the High Roads. He and Steve now made London trips to see them. The Kilburns' sprawling line-up, in all its visual disarray, was hardly as cool as Roxy Music but its musical roughness made a nice change from the power-trio virtuosity so valued in orthodox rock circles. And their bawdy wit contrasted with the confessional school of earnest singer-songwriters.

Highly favoured, also, were an American band called Dan Hicks & His Hot Licks. Unwieldy as the Kilburns, with female vocalists too, they specialised in Western Swing, a sort of vintage cowboy jazz. Like another US outfit, Commander Cody & His Lost Planet Airmen, they subverted hippy culture with a new kind of country-rock that made a deep impression on British pub rock of the early 1970s, chiefly Nick Lowe's band Brinsley Schwarz. Closer to home were Manchester's comedic art-rockers Alberto Y Lost Trios Paranoias, and on the London circuit Chilli Willi & the Red Hot Peppers, Dr Feelgood and the former Faces bassman Ronnie Lane. All were a pre-punk reaction against progressive complexity and chest-beating machismo.

If David Bowie and Roxy Music were unrivalled as art school heroes across the country, in Deaf School's case there was also interest in the harmony acts Manhattan Transfer, Sha Na Na and Britain's own Darts, whose multiple vocalists dressed up in varying styles of retro camp or glamour. A Glaswegian-led group, the Sensational Alex Harvey Band, combined solid thug-rock with extravagant theatrics, while Steve at least still dreamed of slick soul showmen like James Brown, the Temptations and the Four Tops. The Beatles, who had split in 1970, were not role models: in their immediate aftermath a rising generation was inclined to escape their shadow. Especially, perhaps, in Liverpool.

'The band from the Deaf School' were at first a random line-up of rotating frontmen and women, eclectically dressed, preferring skits and wit to musical skill or singer-songwriter sincerity. Joining them was akin to reinventing yourself as a comic character. Most recruits were art students, some were college staff. It's quite possible that some simply wandered in off the street. They were all over the place. Clive Langer was driving the tramcar, but his ad hoc band still had a touch of the Frankensteins.

TWO

Didn't You Have a Beard?

*The Randy Vicar – The Sage of Accrington
– The Portsmouth Sinfonia*

THEY WERE NOT 'DEAF SCHOOL' immediately. 'I wanted to call the band Counterculture,' says Clive. 'But it was just a bit *Guardian*, a bit Hampstead. Or the other name I was pushing for was the Rovers, but it sounded like a folk band.' One of their singers, Sandra, recalls someone suggesting Bex Bissell & the Carpet Sweepers.

Nobody asked about your musical aptitude. Clive Langer:

> The idea behind Deaf School at the beginning was not about choosing people who could play the best. Music was in a frightening state, and normally the people who could play the best were playing bad rock music. So we wanted people who could play enough

to get by, but who looked good or had something very interesting to offer. It was partly through our lack of musical ability that the sound of Deaf School was created.

At that time people's clothing was mainly very boring, it was flared loons and the girls wore dresses that were like curtains, skirts straight from the waist down to the floor, a bit bedraggled. And even glam was coming to an end, or was very commercial. The Kilburns were inspirational in the way they dressed, with old suits. I had a suit made at college with images from *Exchange & Mart* stamped on it, that Steve Hardstaff made for me. And seeing Ian Dury mixing and matching different clothes, I had a demob suit that cost nothing and it looked good with short hair.

The girls were allowed to do whatever they wanted; later the Bright Sisters became a bit more organised but initially there was four or five of them. They were just there because they were girls at college that we fancied or liked.

While they acquired accomplices, Steve and Clive were also writing material. Their first effort, 'Ding Dong', was inspired by the doorbell campaign for Avon cosmetics. Another, 'Wah Ching', was prompted by New York graffiti. Having, as yet, no expectation of making records they wrote songs specifically for live performance. And performance, in their eyes, was not confined to music.

Deaf School's resident man of the cloth, the Reverend Max Ripple, was at this point a young tutor named John Wood. He played a part in admitting several members to the college. And when he joined their rehearsals, inter-band banter acquired a whole new level of theoretical discourse. Let John/Max tell his own story:

> The funny thing is – shock horror – I am a Southerner. Born in the West Country, then moved to London, I always wanted to go to college in the North. When I got into Manchester Art College I was over the moon. I don't know why, because I'd never been north of Watford. One of my first teaching jobs was at Liverpool School of Art, where I met a bunch of people who would eventually become part of Deaf School. I became tutor to Clive Langer and Steve Allen, who heard me playing hymns on an old harmonium and asked me to join them in their quest to 'surf' the unique vibe known as Liverpool. It's a party town, isn't it?
>
> When Deaf School kicked off I was living in Manchester and working in Liverpool. I guess I was apprehensive about commuting, as I could sense that I was crossing tribal boundaries each day. After a while the art school offered us a grand apartment at Number 1, Mossley Hill Drive, which my family and I rented from the university for the princely sum of £11 a week. An amazing place with a ballroom downstairs.
>
> In the last five years a few of us in the band have realised how dyslexic we are. The fact that none of us knew this at the time is a peculiar testament to the art school system. It had no educational agenda, except the implicit invitation to encourage students to learn something, somewhere, somehow. I doubt whether some of us would have survived a traditional university regime. In those days the

average art student's life was measured out in pints, rather than in coffee spoons. Indeed, the state grant was generous and the Philharmonic was a veritable temple of learning.

Liverpool 8 was a bit hairy at that time. I'd heard it might be a bit rough, and of course, you tend to see what you're expecting to see. The first night I moved in I remember waiting outside a phone box. The couple making the call were being terrorised by two scallies who kept opening the door and demanding money in a menacing way. When I got into the phone box I soon realised it would be hard to shake them off. Pretty soon, the situation escalated and I found one of them hanging on my arm and kicking my leg as hard as he could. I was determined to stand my ground, manfully, but as a card-carrying, wishy-washy liberal, was reluctant to box their ears. I think they were about six or seven years old. Just then, I saw a guy running down Princes Road, armed with a spear. He was chasing two girls. Welcome to Liverpool!

There was a lot of poverty. As a student, Steve Allen lived in Smithdown Road. If he had to leave the flat, he'd look out of the window to see if any dogs were there. You'd need a good head start on the pack. These were not ragamuffin pets; they were feral beasts that would rip you open and finish you, if given the chance. In hindsight, these experiences may have been more useful to Steve than art school. Certainly a good training for his subsequent career as A&R man at Warner Brothers. You forget these things as life gets softer, but Liverpool was quite tough in some ways. It was certainly an eye-opener for me. As a soft kid from the South, I was naive in every way.

I've loved pianos since I was two or three, when I can remember climbing onto the stool and pressing my fists down onto the keyboard. This inspired my first theory of how a piano works. Basically, you push down those black-and-white things and the room tells you which ones to push down next. It's not a sophisticated hypothesis, but it makes more sense than the bollocks they teach you in physics.

This is as near as I ever got to a formal education as a performer. Since 1967 I had thought of myself as an artist who built electronic circuits. This was the era of conceptual art. Somebody recently said that my early electronic work was quite like Brian Eno's, which I'd never thought of, but I can see what he meant. My circuits were supposed to be digital but actually had so many leaky components that the sounds they generated were chaotic and unpredictable. In a way, they were musical systems that improvised new patterns based on their current situation. But my interest was as much in sound as it was in music.

Like most of us in the band, I couldn't read music when we met, and still can't. I guess we got away with it because we saw Deaf School as a theatrical experiment, rather than as professional music. The name 'Deaf School' made me feel at home. Compared with other bands at that time I think we were gloriously inept. But age did seem a big concern at the time. I was ancient, I was 27 and I think Clive was very concerned that we had an old-timer in the band.

There is some precious cine-footage of early Deaf School rehearsing in a college basement studio. We see Max, the art lecturer, expounding at length, while the other musicians are crouched purposefully over their instruments, awaiting the count-in. 'It really shows the development of the band,' says Steve Allen, 'with Clive the leader. And Max is still trying to take it into performance art: "What are we actually trying to *achieve* here? It's all very well saying 'Let's just play the song,' Clive, but what is the song *about*?" If a song went from, say, A major to A minor John would say, "Excuse me, could you remind me again, what is a major?" And we thought he was joking. But Clive would show him what to do.'

∗∗∗

An important addition was another from that class of '73, Steve Lindsey, whom we shall soon know as Mr Average. 'I went to art college,' he said a few years later, 'because I wanted to be a musician, which may sound strange but isn't. You only go to music college if you want to play classical music, but if you want to play rock'n'roll I think you've got to be more of an artist than an actual technical wizard. Pop music is about reflecting cultures and that is very much the same with modern art.'

If not an actual Scouser, he was at least from Merseyside, raised in Bebington on the Wirral bank of the river. He now describes himself as 'a very mediocre art talent':

I was lucky. I must have done well in my foundation

course at Chester, I really wanted to get in to Liverpool because they did animation and film and TV. And I actually got in without having the requisite number of A-levels. So I was a year younger than the likes of Clive and Steve, I entered Liverpool at 18 when most other people around me were at least 19.

My dad used to be a semi-pro drummer; my earliest memories are of him going out three or four times a week doing gigs, dinner dances in places like Litherland Town Hall or Chester Country Club, or the pit of the Liverpool Empire. When the Merseybeat thing took off he'd be doing dances alongside the Beatles and Gerry & the Pacemakers. When he did a gig on the *Royal Iris*, the Beatles said, 'Excuse me Mr Lindsey, d'you mind if you move your drums a bit so we can get our amps in?'

My dad would occasionally not have a bass in his band – it was sax, drums, piano, something like that – so I'd quietly sit in at the back, just thumping the bass, feeling my way around these tunes.

When I was 11 I got to know this guy at our junior school called Ted Robbins, whose mother was related to Paul McCartney. So Ted and I became friends and I got to know the family, and Ted's sister Kate Robbins. In fact the band I was in before anything else happened was called Queen! That was me gigging with Kate Robbins and a couple of schoolmates at rugby clubs and stuff. I then went out with Jane Robbins, another one of the sisters, for many years and all through the Deaf School period.

At the art college I felt out of my depth because

I was a year younger. But I knew that going to art college was the best place to get into a band, and within a few weeks – the course had started in late September – the word had gone out that there was a band rehearsing in the prefabs at Myrtle Street [another annexe, off Hope Street]. I thought, 'Oh yeah, I wouldn't mind a little bit of that.'

The Myrtle Street branch was where I was based, doing graphics. I never rehearsed at the Deaf School. 'Who's this band? What are they called?' 'Oh, I dunno, but they're from the Deaf School.' The band was any number of people, whoever happened to be passing by or had an instrument. I'm not sure how many times they'd met before rehearsals moved to Myrtle Street. I brought this cheapo bass guitar with me. Clive and Steve had a few songs up their sleeves and John [Max Ripple] had written a few interesting instrumentals, 1930s type things. There was this unbelievable array of people who would just come and go. Play a few notes on a flugelhorn. Or the banjo. It was a nebulous thing.

The only focus was aiming for the Christmas dance, at the refectory in Hope Street. So we had an aim, and we knew that we'd need a set of songs. And Clive being the way that Clive is, he basically MD'd it. And I think I was in because I was a reliable plodding bass-player, rather than a fly-by-night. It was what they needed. And those few weeks up to Christmas flew by. We got material together. It was a real melting pot of ideas from all sorts of people.

***

At the back was their drummer Tim Whittaker. Born in 1952, Tim was of the college intake two years above Clive and Steve. Raised in Accrington, he spoke in the broad Lancastrian accent which Scousers mock as 'woollyback'. But in the cosmopolitan world of an art college he was quite at home. Clive recalls he was a not a great drummer, at least to begin with, but was taken on at the band's second-ever rehearsal because they preferred him to a more competent hard rock drummer who'd preceded him

'Tim was fabulous,' says Anne Martin, a girl in their circle who would soon find another name. 'Hilarious. In his studio at the art school he'd have these three canvases set up, right up to the picture rail and every day he'd do three paintings.

> He was always covered in paint, and he'd have his books, these medical dictionaries, then he'd screen-print horrible, hideous afflictions, ghastly. He was mad, completely bonkers. When I shared a flat with him he had this really nice girlfriend, Ziggy, who was Lithuanian. Her parents used to send her pork scratchings before you could buy them here, and sometimes he'd miss the parcel and it would go to the post office They'd go and get this greasy old parcel and be eating these porky pieces that had been hanging around for three weeks.

> So they were an item and then Tim's mother came and poor Ziggy had to disappear because Tim's mother ran a bridal shop in Oswaldtwistle. It's quite extraordinary that he was intimidated by his mother. Tim had an exhibition at the library in Oswaldtwistle and we all went.

The most dedicated painter in the band, Whittaker was much loved by Deaf School, and much mourned upon his untimely death in 1996. Bryan Biggs, a year below him at the college, had a studio on the same floor as Tim's and recalls that 'he was doing these very large, American-influenced paintings, very vigorous. He walked around like Jackson Pollock, his jeans splattered with paint. So he really lived the life. They weren't abstract, they were figurative, but done with the vigour of the abstract expressionists. A very nice guy, very funny, with his thick Lancashire accent.'

'Tim was always murder to get out of bed,' says the band's eventual road manager Ken Testi. 'We'd always leave him till last to be picked up, but it wasn't unusual for the whole band to be sitting outside Tim's flat for 45 minutes. And me with bleeding knuckles trying to get him to open the door. Couldn't wake him.'

We can at least let Tim Whittaker speak for himself. Writing in a Deaf School edition of Roger Eagle's fanzine *The Last Trumpet*, he wrote the following auto-profile:

A lot of the time I spend holding a stick made of wood in either hand hitting plastic stuff stretched over wood. This makes a loud noise which sometimes annoys people and I also hit big metal things which crash loudly. This also annoys people. If I am clever at what I hit and when, and also if somebody plays a guitar loudly at the same time, this makes a difference and mainly people like it. But sometimes it still annoys some people...

I like dancing, I like to shake my arms and head about and move my feet in wild abandon, but to do this I must be very drunk. But when I'm drunk I can't dance and I fall on the floor. This can be very unromantic...

By way of elaboration he added two poems:

> 1.
> *If I had a dog I would call it Geoffrey*
> *If I had a cat I would call it Neil*
> *If I had a goldfish I would call it Marlene*
> *If I had a horse I would call it Alan*
> *If I had a rabbit I would call it Christine*
> *If I had a brain I would call this madness.*
>
> 2.
> *Sad is wet*
> *Happy is dry*
> *When you cry*
> *You are wet.*

* * *

During that first term, on the same coach trip to Blackpool that saw Steve and Clive develop their friendship and dream a few dreams, there was an older student named Sam Davis. He was from Oldbury, by West Bromwich in the Black Country: 'And he talked like that,' says his widow Joan (Sam died in 2010). 'But when he came to Liverpool he said he got rid of the accent, because it didn't pull any birds.' At 18 he'd done his pre-Dip at Aston University and came to Liverpool in 1971. He lived there for the rest of his life.

'There's a bit of a story,' he said in a 1994 interview with Kevin McManus:

Clive was in his first year then. I'd come across him in my final year. Every year the art college used to have these trips to Blackpool, which was just an excuse to get pissed. And on this long trip that particular year there was me and a couple of blokes organising it and Clive came and complained to us because he thought there were not enough first years getting seats on the coach. So that was my first contact, we sorted it out and he came to Blackpool.

And that night, I was going along the front in one of those horse-drawn carriages, totally off my head, standing up making this speech. Unbeknown to me I'd gone past Clive and he thought, 'Hmm, he's quite good as a performer.'

The band was getting together in this studio space, we used to call them sheds, in Myrtle Street at the back of the college. I used to cut through there to go to the Caledonia pub and I started hearing bits of noise coming out of this shed. I was sitting in the Caledonia one night and Clive came over and said we want you to sing this song. And that's basically how I got involved with the band. I never thought of myself being in a band, I always thought of myself as a serious artist.

Basically, if you fancied being in it you were in it, provided you turned up to rehearsals, that was the premise. I suppose we thought of it as being art college, it wasn't mainstream. Nobody could play very well early on but I think Clive's intention was to improve that aspect of it. And the more you play the better you get.

In Clive's eyes, Sam was 'a character, one of the older guys who looked cool. He was gagging to get into a band, and I was the one who could start a band.' Sam was anyway part of the social set coalescing around Deaf School. Among them was Anne Martin: 'The first time I ever met Sam, I went to the Cracke, when I first came to Liverpool. I was 18 and I said to Sam, "Hi," but he had chicken pox and I caught chicken pox and I got this summer job and I was quite ill. But then I did share a flat with Sam and he was quite scary in the early days. He used to get his grant and go crazy, he was quite wild. But a fabulous person.'

Sam, for all his carousing in the pubs of Liverpool 8 and impromptu performances by the light of the Blackpool illuminations, spoke in a wonderfully soft voice. In Deaf School he adopted the name Eric Shark, with its vaguely *West Side Story* connotations. 'Good for signing autographs,' he murmured.

As well as John Wood, another teacher in the early line-up was Roy Holt, from Sutton in the Surrey suburbs of London; he'd arrived at Liverpool via the Royal Academy. Among the 1973 intake interviewed by Roy was a Fine Arts applicant, Sandra Harris, a Liverpool girl who had done her foundation year at the college itself. 'Roy was one of the friendlier ones,' says Sandra, 'just a nice guy where the others were off-hand. He would have been about 31 then.' Her own entanglement with Deaf School was not long in coming. A friend who painted with her in those well-lit upstairs studios shared a flat in Sefton Park with Clive Langer. And Sandra was soon going out with Roy Holt. When Roy invited her along to the nascent band's rehearsals, both in Hope Street and the Deaf School annexe, she says: 'It was like, Could I actually sing? I'd only really sung in school.' But she gave it a go. After all, that was the Deaf School way.

* * *

Fast becoming another aspect of the Deaf School way was the adoption of personas, or stage personalities. It was never a formal policy – they were a band, not a theatre troupe – and not everyone did it. But many did devise alter-egos, as if creating an individual artwork. The retiring Clive Langer, whose own reinvention went no further than 'Cliff Hanger', stood out by dint of his serious and watchful demeanour. His spectacles marked him apart as the band's thinker – rather like the character in prison movies who gets called 'the Prof'.

But his intention was slightly different. 'It was easy for me,' he says, 'because I could be Buddy Holly, rock guitarist, so my persona was the history of pop, as opposed to something from outside the rock world. With the name Cliff you suddenly think rock'n'roll. So I did have a persona and I wanted a quiff, but my hair wasn't right. I'm still trying. That's who I was in the band, I wanted to be the rocker.'

It's curious how, in conversation with Deaf School members, they refer to one another using real names or stage names, seemingly at random, and even switch in mid-sentence. 'I think we all flip,' agrees the Reverend Max, 'even in emails to each other.

It's a curious thing. My persona – 'altar ego', get it? – evolved as part of our resistance to the standard pseudo-American style that most British bands were keen to cultivate at the time. On a personal level I was also sending up the church, as I had a couple of uncles who were vicars. My grandmother had been a missionary in Africa. When all other bands seemed to be wearing blue denim and doing power chords, the idea of having a Church of England vicar in a rock band seemed hilarious to me. I guess we all are playing versions of ourselves, to some extent. You play up to your weaknesses and it becomes funny.

His choice of name was partly a nod to the music hall heroes Max Miller and Max Wall, but was directly lifted from the technical inscription, 'max ripple' (or maximum ripple current) found on the old TVs he used for sound sculptures. 'That's part of the character of Max Ripple. It's an empty space. Innocuous. Albie Donnelly [of the Liverpool band Supercharge] saw me in baggy suit and vicar's things and he said, "Don't suppose yer get many shags dressed like that, do yer?"' (We might reserve judgement on this matter. A female pop reporter of the time wrote: 'The Reverend is virginal only when he dons his dog collar... Girls beware. If ever he says to you "To the woods to the woods", just scoot!')

Enrico Cadillac Jnr thinks his persona dates from a routine they did in early shows that began with him pretending to be an audience member, as Sam asked for volunteers to join them on stage. Since he had the seedy Latin gigolo look prepared he improvised a suitable name. (To this day he will seldom enter the stage from a conventional direction if any alternative is possible.)

Frankie Average, alias Steve Lindsey, has a more elaborate back story:

On my first day at college in Chester, I would have been 17, I said, 'Hi, my name's Steve.' This older guy said, 'No, I don't like that name, I'll call you Frank.' Thanks to this random act, throughout college I was Frank. Then I went to Liverpool. As part of Deaf School's evolution and this notion of having a persona, I remember John [that is, Max] coming in to a rehearsal, 'Yeah, I've got my name now.' At that point in art college I felt really thrown in at the deep end: 'What am I doing here? Who are all these clever people around me?' All these questions that you ask yourself at that age.

I thought of the miles and miles of semi-detached houses in Bebington where I'm from. 'I'm just so fucking average!' So that's where Frankie Average came from. Also around that time there were adverts in the press for stuff like Burtons suits: 'Don't be Mr Average, get one of our suits made specially.' So I named myself that. It wasn't anyone trying to insult me, it was my own invention.

For his costume Average hit upon a collarless suit, from the Fab Four's Pierre Cardin period. He took advantage of a common art school perk in having someone run it up for him:

I was a big Beatles fan but by that time it was seen as an ironic statement. A guy in Fashion & Textiles made it as part of his degree. I had to go into the class and be measured for the suit with all the people around. Very embarrassing. The tutor was there, going, 'You measure from the nape of the neck, down to the coccyx,' and I had a handkerchief

> bulging in my pocket and he says, 'As we can see,
> this gentleman dresses on the left!'

As new members came aboard they inevitably brought their own tastes into the mixture, whether it was Steve Lindsey's crafted pop sensibility or Roy Holt's love for vintage tea-room foxtrots. But Clive was the musical director, and among his own influences was a highly important force in Deaf School's evolution. Unlikely as it seems, this was a massive classical ensemble of consciously inexpert players called the Portsmouth Sinfonia.

***

The Portsmouth concept reached Liverpool in several ways. One source was a 24-year-old tutor called Steve Hardstaff, who came to the college in 1969. A music obsessive himself, he taught several members of Deaf School and his design input became intrinsic to the whole project. (His artwork has since served everyone from Led Zeppelin to Half Man Half Biscuit.) Hardstaff had studied at Portsmouth, while teaching at Falmouth, and met Sinfonia people at both.

The Sinfonia was launched at Portsmouth art college in 1970. The idea was to combine musicians of all ability levels, some playing instruments unfamiliar to them, whose 'inevitable, unforced errors' would bring a fresh element of random creativity. The composer Gavin Bryars joined the conductor John Farley, and an early ally was Roxy Music's Brian Eno, who produced the Sinfonia's first two albums. Billed by their publicist as 'the world's worst orchestra', they achieved an ironic cult following sufficient to get a booking at the Albert Hall. One speciality was a medley (or 'mudley') of popular classics including the *William Tell Overture.*

Sinfonia 'grouplets' sprang up everywhere, and lectures were given at Liverpool art college. David Saunders, then a tutor both at Portsmouth and Liverpool, takes up the story:

I suppose I wasn't a very good teacher, because I was interested in people who wanted to change the system. I was an iconoclast, really. I was just about the only visual artist who was interested in experimental music, and I was encouraging this sort of thing. The Sinfonia spawned little bands all over the place. Michael Nyman [the composer] taught at Trent Polytechnic art school and he had a band there; there would be art school grouplets in Liverpool and Nottingham, an amazing time. It seemed to me that most of the creativity was in this field of experimental music.

And Brian [Eno] was in his final year at Winchester, but when he got wind of what was happening in Portsmouth, where you had all the big names teaching, he used to come over and I remember him saying to me, 'I know how to make a band that will get to Number 1 and I can do it in six months.' And he did. Well, 'Virginia Plain' was certainly a big hit.

I could hardly play a note, but I was invited by Deaf School right at the very start, in 1973. I had a tenor horn which belonged to the Portsmouth Sinfonia and I played that at every gig. Of course it wasn't much seen in pop music or for that matter in classical music. It made a very strange sound. Clive was quite a disciplinarian, really. I said to him once, 'I can't play this, Clive, I'm just not good enough.' I was always terrified every time I had to do a gig! But one night they all said to me, 'Oh Dave, that sounded wonderful.' But the mistakes were always there.

Having co-opted Saunders into Deaf School, Clive was duly invited to join the Portsmouth Sinfonia:

Dave and I were talking and I said, 'I've got a flute,' and he said, 'Come and join us, it'll be fun.' So I joined the Portsmouth Sinfonia late on but I did the Albert Hall, got on the first album cover. I'm on the picture on the back of the album, the first album I'd ever been on.

It influenced Deaf School in the sense that 'It doesn't matter if you can play or not.' Average could play, and Ian [Ritchie, saxophonist] could play, but the rest of us couldn't. Well, I could play but only in my own terms, whereas they were capable of playing anything. John is like a pub pianist, he'll hear a song and play it, but when you say to him, go to G, he's still like 'What?' He'd learn things just by listening. So the whole Portsmouth Sinfonia concept was an influence, and a bit of fun I did on the side, and met a few people. And Eno was there, which was exciting.

To this day, he credits the Portsmouth Sinfonia as validating Deaf School's choice of name – which would soon prove controversial – for its implication that they were unembarrassed by any disability. His colleague Enrico approved:

We can't forget the importance of the Portsmouth Sinfonia. Deaf School didn't come out of it but it was a parallel idea, that we weren't going to have any musos in our band. It wouldn't stop someone if they were right in other ways, but we were looking for interesting characters and people with a talent for whatever it was – performance art, lyrics, poetry. We weren't looking for good singers or good players, and the Portsmouth Sinfonia was basically made up of non-qualified musicians. It goes along with Brian Eno's idea of recording, where he doesn't want anyone to hear what the other guy's playing in the studio. See what comes out of it. It's normally a mess, but he'll find something in there. That colliding atoms idea.

Max Ripple, though not a Sinfonia member, was naturally attracted to its exaltation of the amateur:

I think that's true. It was our disclaimer, our way of excusing ourselves. The politics of the Portsmouth Sinfonia are a sort of Utopian idea that everyone can play. It's a bit like Rudolf Laban, the dance choreographer who liberated the whole thing by saying 'Anything can be dance.' An eyebrow movement can be dance.

* * *

A born organiser, Clive Langer became the college's social secretary in his first term and ensured that Deaf School, the band he had nurtured for nearly three months, would debut at the Hope Street Christmas dance. As Steve Allen says, 'We only got together to do the Christmas party.

That was the idea. But knowing Clive better now, I realise he had further plans. There were at least four tutors in the band on stage playing French horn, flugelhorn, all different instruments. That first gig was probably the closest it got to the Portsmouth Sinfonia. It was crazy, and absolutely rammed. We were amazed.'

Steve Hardstaff remembers it as taking place on a Friday night just before the Christmas break:

> I got horribly pissed. It was chaotic and fun. I hate to use the word 'happening' but it was really more of an event than just a dance. There were more people on the stage than in the audience because the world and his wife were in the band. It was jam-packed because the art school dances were legendary. I don't think anyone was allowed to sell alcohol, so the drink was free, which was of course a recipe for drunken hedonism. Those things weren't designed to make money, I think the Students Union got a budget and just blew it.

Average: 'There was a guy called Nigel [Helyer, a student member of the early Deaf School, who later relocated to Australia and specialised in sound sculpture]; he sang a few songs at the Christmas gig, and he'd moulded a rubberised body-cast, in which he did the whole gig, very arty. There was any number of girls and any number of musicians.'

It's uncertain exactly which girls appeared. Subsequent Bright Sisters (as the female vocal troupe was dubbed) express doubt whether they were involved. Nor was there a stage as such, only a shoving aside of canteen tables. According to his brother Phil (who saw the band's first rehearsal, back at the Deaf School), Steve Allen wore a straw boater with a striped T-shirt and baggy white bell-bottoms. His Clark Gable moustache was already emerging. There were also, in the melee, a violinist and 'a guy in a full frogman's suit with the hat on. After the gig he was choking to death and they were trying to cut it off him: "I can't breathe!"'

Sam Davis would recall the Christmas show as 'a great success, because we were all dressed up and there were loads of fashion students there.' Enrico Cadillac adds, 'I remember people saying how great the gig was. It was fun, and people kept coming up and we made a special connection with the girls in the Fashion & Textiles. So that was kind of where it got started, us thinking, Well, maybe we should do this again.'

Bryan Biggs, their fellow student (and nowadays Artistic Director of Liverpool's arts centre, the Bluecoat), thrilled to that show and made posters and backdrops for other Deaf School gigs, with themes including a Bay City Rollers take-off and a Donald McGill-style seaside postcard:

There were a lot of them, probably about 15, but I can remember people who lasted only one gig. They were the archetypal art school band, doing all the clichés: they used the building for rehearsals and gigs, they used the graphic department to make the posters, while the fashion department helped develop the look. There were fashion and textile students in the audience who would dress up the way the band would dress up. So there was a real synergy.

I felt the band was informed by a degree of critical art discourse, though art schools then were generally still more about learning skills, not a lot of theory.

But we all knew about Duchamp, for instance, and conceptual art was in the magazines. Plus the fact that someone from the Portsmouth Sinfonia comes to give a lecture at the Deaf School and inspires the formation of a band positions them in the context of a twentieth-century avant-garde. There was some grounding in art history. Pop art was definitely there. And in my first year it seemed everybody was knocked out by the Roxy Music album, which had come out earlier.

Clive was brilliant. He led them into becoming a music band as opposed to an art project. Although as an art project it was interesting, because no one apart from Portsmouth Sinfonia was really doing what they were doing: the whole idea that you didn't need to be able to play.

In their own way, Deaf School were punk *avant la lettre*, at a time when musical virtuosity was highly regarded, even among pub bands. Deaf School's attitude was heretical in 1973. They were truly a band out of time. And frequently out of tune.

✳ ✳ ✳

Looking back in 1975, Bryan Ferry told the *New York Times*: 'In England, the kids with the most style and the ones most into our music come from places like Liverpool, Birmingham and Newcastle.' Roxy Music's first album was released in June 1972. By the time of the art school Christmas dance, in December 1973, they had made two more, *For Your Pleasure* and *Stranded*. And in October, Ferry had unveiled a solo LP of cover versions, *These*

Foolish Things. The stylish kids of those provincial cities were getting plenty to chew on.

Also in October 1973, just before Deaf School's stage debut, Bowie released his own LP of cover versions, *Pin-Ups.* At the same time he played his *1980 Floor Show* at the London Marquee club, in which Marianne Faithfull vamped up in full 1930s style for Noel Coward's '20th Century Blues', and Bowie himself tackled two Liverpool faves, the Merseys' 'Sorrow' and the Mojos' 'Everything's Alright'. The Beatles' reign over British pop had recently expired, and with it died a notion that rock would always move forward along a continuum that never looked back. Bowie and Ferry, by contrast, suggested pop as an eternal present, a postmodern mixture of nostalgic futurism and futuristic nostalgia.

'Didn't you have a beard?' is the waspish enquiry in Deaf School's 'Hi Jo Hi'. 'Weren't you kind of weird?' It was a time to re-draw some of fashion's battle-lines. Down in London, in September 1973, the decade-defining Biba boutique moved into its final and grandest home, the converted Derry & Tom's store in Kensington High Street.

Deaf School in Liverpool, and others around the country, absorbed the new aesthetic almost subliminally. The vintage glamour of the 1940s and the rock'n'roll flash of the 1950s were seized upon greedily, because they opposed the hippy 1960s reverence for all things natural. As the denim-boys' beards fell from favour, and the cooler girls ditched their maidenly medieval cheesecloths, there was a move towards artifice, synthetic materials, harsh colours, a certain decadence with undertones of cruelty. From this sensibility came the originators of London punk. For Deaf School, 200 miles away, punk was to prove problematic.

THREE

'It Was the Death of the Loon'

A Room With No View – Introducing Miss Bette Bright – The Melody Maker's Fatal Embrace

DEAF SCHOOL'S SOCIAL LIFE favoured the same circuit that the Liverpool Scene had known. 'They were not really around the art college by now,' says Average, 'and they would have been seen by us as a generation older. But we used to hang around the Everyman Bistro a lot and the likes of Mike McGear/McCartney, and Adrian Henri would be figures around town.' And wherever Adrian Henri was, there was often his young Glaswegian girlfriend Carol Ann Duffy, the future poet laureate, who spent the mid-1970s studying philosophy at Liverpool University.

Clive recalls, 'We were regulars at Peter Kavanagh's [alias the Grapes, off Catharine Street], where the tutors from the art school went, either there or the Cracke or the Phil.' And Enrico:

> Chauffeurs [a private members' club at 60 Hope Street] re-opened around the time we were there, but it wasn't really our scene. We were much more in the Phil or the Belvedere. The Belvedere's lovely. And the Cracke, obviously. Or we'd go in the Casablanca, 'the Caz'. And at night we were invariably in the Gladray [where strippers danced to the juke-box] on Upper Parliament Street. Clive thought that was incredibly romantic. I took him there and to the Somali [a basement drinking den in the same street] which I called S. O'Malley's. The guys who worked there were seven foot tall and they had to crouch down to let you in the door. A lot of the art students went there. Wherever the girls from Fashion & Textiles were going, you'd gravitate towards that.

Even more important was O'Connor's Tavern, half-way down Hardman Street. Formerly a synagogue and later a morgue, O'Connor's had ominously few windows and resembled a Wild West saloon. Its upstairs room, with no view whatsoever, had hosted music and poetry since 1967 and it features on the cover of the Liverpool Scene's 1968 LP *Amazing Adventures Of*, where Adrian Henri and his crowd (bearded or mini-skirted) surround the portly, bow-tied landlord Jimmy Moore. A year or so afterwards, gigs were staged there by the future doyenne of Eric's, Doreen Allen, and by Henri's saxophonist Mike Evans: his bookings took in a novice comedian called Alexei Sayle and an ambitious boy in glasses named Declan MacManus, eventually re-styled Elvis Costello.

Rather earlier, Mike Evans even took Yoko Ono for a drink there.

Within Deaf School's lifetime the in-crowd baton passed across the road to a bakery-turned-wine bar called Kirkland's, but in 1974 O'Connor's was still bohemia's frontier garrison, a passing-point for anyone venturing uphill from central Liverpool. In spring that year Deaf School played their first gigs outside the art college here. The pub's standard fare was nothing special. Beat poetry's hey-day was over and local live music meant gruff hippy bands doing folk-rock or blues boogie. Even so, it was a sanctuary from the hard conformist vibe of aggressively white, downtown Scouseland with its gangster-owned 'no-jeans-or-trainers' cabaret clubs.

Buoyed by the success of their Christmas debut and a few more Hope Street appearances, the amorphous collective were excited by the chance to perform for a slightly wider crowd. It was still the case, Enrico says, that 'anyone could get on stage if they wanted to'. Average recalls that they remained in thrall to the retro element:

> There was a section of the gig that was fenced off for 'the Essoldo Cinema Orchestra' [the Essoldo was a picture house chain, its kitsch connotations of suburban art deco precisely echoing 'Roxy']. It was a kind of interlude where the rock'n'roll members of the band would put our Essoldo hats on and do these rumpty-tump 1930s tunes. So we'd be doing rock'n'roll stuff, Clive banging away on his Telecaster, doing crazy, punky-type stuff, before any of that was a twinkle in anyone's eyes, and the next minute we go into *that*. Brilliant. At that point Enrico was just one of the singers, and it was great fun, a party.

At O'Connor's they played freshly written numbers like 'Searching For a Home' and 'Guess Who's Coming to Dinner', both calypso-ska in feel with an eerie foretaste of Madness. If the sound was rudimentary the dress code was not. 'From the earliest days,' says Enrico, 'we used to change from our street clothes. That was an unwritten rule, we never performed on stage in our street clothes.' They made an exception one night for a special show as the Diggers, dressed in denims. Cine-footage shows Eric Shark inviting a *faux*-reluctant Steve Allen to the microphone: as the band revs up to a tender ballad named 'Dreamboat Belle', he shyly announces his new name, Enrico Cadillac Jnr. They would never wear denim again.

As Max Ripple observes: 'Steve/Enrico had a genius touch with his anti-superstar trick. At O'Connor's I would just start this song, ching-ching-ching, clichéd entry, and then someone would say, "Is Enrico in the house?" And he'd appear quite bashfully in the background and he'd have to be pushed on to perform his song, like he was too shy, which I thought was a fantastic reversal of the rock idea.'

The Enrico look was budget Hollywood. The early 1970s was a golden age of influential cinema, and no art student would be unaware of *American Graffiti*, the *Godfather* films, *A Clockwork Orange*, *Cabaret*, *The Great Gatsby* or *The Rocky Horror Show*. Most of these found some echo in popular music, including Deaf School, wherever the denim-and-beards aesthetic was being rejected. Deaf School's sheer diversity was either a strength or a weakness, depending on your sympathies.

As Average notes: 'Clive used to sing quite a few songs in the early days, with his London accent, and it sounded really good. And in the nature of college there were lots of people from all over the place congregating there. So there was a multitude of accents. Sam was from the West Midlands, but the nature of his delivery was kind of American, though it didn't sound forced.'

Max agrees there was a retro impulse at work, though he feels its spirit was essentially English: 'There was a sort of nostalgia, but it was more John Betjeman. What I remember of Clive's paintings was that Ivon Hitchens was one of his idols, so he painted stuff with the same sensibility, very romantic but in a strong tradition of the English garden, of nature being open. So I think that looseness is wanting to be rock'n'roll, but not wanting to be American, not wanting to be West Coast.'

Their following was still an art school one, but playing outside of Hope Street presented new challenges, as the band's resident man of God remembers: 'There was no changing room at O'Connor's and I was sorting out some make-up, with my vicar's collar on and baggy suit, combing my hair in the mirror of a Morris 1000 van at the side of the road. These two labourers who had obviously just come out of the pub looked at me and one goes, "Eh *Faa*-ther, come 'ere!" and I ran around the corner and back into O'Connor's thinking, Oh Jesus, they're going to beat me up.'

***

A friend from college was Kevin Ward, who was taught by Steve Hardstaff and soon joined him in making extra-curricular use of the print-shop facilities on Deaf School's behalf. He'd fallen for them immediately:

Art colleges were just the most amazing places in those days, full of people with original ideas. At the time Deaf School started I was sharing a flat in Princes Avenue with Sam. They were a complete shambles, but everyone at the college loved them. The other bands, who played hard rock, couldn't see it at all. They thought it was stupid, whimsical rubbish. And technically Deaf School were still nowhere. But they had this magic about them.

Kevin Ward's artwork would, in time, produce some definitive Deaf School images. But, for now, he made an even more compelling contribution. Having no musical ambitions himself, he brought his girlfriend along to watch a few rehearsals. His girlfriend, Anne Martin, had strong show business roots, and something in Deaf School awakened her performing instincts. Enrico thinks they were probably scouting for someone to partner Sandra Harris on vocals. Whatever the case, no sooner had Deaf School started their short O'Connor's residency than Anne was a member.

'I wasn't at the art school,' says the future Bette Bright. 'I was going to go to Reading University, and then I decided to go up to Liverpool because I knew some people there.

I did voluntary work for a year, then I ended up doing an art teaching course [at Notre Dame, at the other end of Hope Street]. I was living in a flat with about five people, including Tim Whittaker. Sam lived there, but later on. I was going out with Kevin, and I went on the trip to Blackpool. And I knew Clive because he had been at Canterbury doing his foundation, and used to work in a restaurant belonging to my cousin, so we made a connection.

So I met them all on this Blackpool trip. And I can't exactly remember how, but Clive somehow knew that my mum had been a tap-dancer, and I think initially I was asked to join the band to be a tap-dancer. Because there was a funny little cabaret ish song which Steve did, that I sang, but we never actually did the tap-dancing. It's all rather vague, because in those days there were so many people in the band. It was enormous and there was Connie, Sandra, a girl called Joan, and then myself, singing.

It was pretty shambolic because there were so many diverse factions in that band. I think there were about 20 people at that point. Every time we did a new show it seemed like a new set. And Steve Allen was always amazing. He was just born to perform. He took after his dad.

But Anne, too, had entertainment in her blood. From Whitstable in Kent, she was the daughter of a noted variety hall turn:

My mother [Christina] was a tap dancer with her two sisters. They were called the Catherine Dunne Trio. They used to work with the Crazy Gang and all those people, she was really glamorous. They would work in the Empire theatres, going around with all the acts. And in fact she was managed by Lew Grade [Britain's most famous impresario and TV mogul of the time]. They were quite crazy, some of the stories they told. They worked in Paris quite a bit and they'd get all their food on a tab at this Russian bistro, and get all their clothes made, they'd have their eyelashes made from their hair. But they'd have no money so they'd settle up when they could. She would do Russian dancing, on roller skates, on a pitched stage. Imagine!

Theatre bills of the 1940s, in fact, reveal the Dunne sisters sharing stages with such luminaries as dance-band singer Sam Browne, 'Jose Marino & Assistant' and Issy Bonn ('the Famous Hebrew Comedian'), who can be seen between Paul and George on the *Sgt. Pepper* cover.

My mother was quite unusual because she had my sister and me when she was in her 40s. So she'd had a whole life. My father worked at BP, he was a clever person, but she was hilarious. If she had to go to cocktail parties and talk to someone who was really boring... she once handed this man her glasses and did a cartwheel, then it was, 'As you were saying?' She was a real character.

Was it her mother who gave Anne a desire to perform?

Possibly. Nothing shocked her. It wasn't as if she went, 'You've *got* to go on the stage,' whereas her older sister sent both of her children to stage schools. In fact the older sister was in the Follies, she was a captain in the Follies before she had the act with my Mum. This old aunt, she never moved off centre stage. She lived to be 90-odd and was quite a witch really, quite poisonous. She wasn't like my Mum.

Like her fellow Southerner John Wood/Max Ripple, Anne found the move to Liverpool a cultural eye-opener:

I lived in Princes Avenue. I loved the way it was so different from where I'd come from. I remember going to Scottie Road and they were selling second-hand false teeth. And it's also quite small, Liverpool, you'd get to know people. At that time there were still bombsites, the Rialto was on the corner. I remember before the riots kicked off, the police often coming and you'd get kids joy-riding cars round there and they'd randomly pick kids up off the street.

I was on the dole but I was supposed to be this community volunteer. I was doing stuff like going round finding out if these old people were still alive, for the social services, this kind of thing. And these people I was working for said, 'Oh, just sign on, it's fine, you're a volunteer.' The next thing, I get summoned to an awful DHSS place, the worst DHSS place in the world, and they offered me a job! I mean, nobody had jobs in Liverpool in those days. I turned it down, so then they offered me another one, and then I was struck off, and the people I worked for started paying me. Six pounds a week or something. I just thought it was ironic that I was offered work in Liverpool.

A recognisable Deaf School line-up was taking shape.

**

Among the next year's art college intake, September 1974, was a girl from the Midlands called Hazel Bartram. Having done her foundation course in Loughborough, she was attracted to Liverpool by the chance to combine sonic and visual elements in her course. And she was interviewed by

Max Ripple (in his secular guise of John Wood, of course) who invited her to join the Deaf School collective. To their sound she added flugelhorn and E-flat tenor horn; to their look she added flapper-girl glamour. She was a solidly trained and experienced player, but even Hazel had sometimes to sit the number out and simply be part of the band's *tableau vivant*. As well as in Deaf School she played for a performance art offshoot of the Portsmouth Sinfonia, the Edge Hill Players, with her Liverpool tutors James Lampard and Dave Saunders, who says of her: 'Hazel was very good. She was an exceptional musician and could play all the things that I couldn't play.'

The next recruit was also a horn player, filling out the Deaf School sound in a more formalised way than was hitherto the case. Ian Ritchie was a Scot born and bred, but when his father's work took the family to Parbold in Lancashire, Liverpool became Ian's nearest university and he applied there to study chemistry.

> I played bugle in the Boys Brigade; at 15 my Dad got me a clarinet and said I should get some lessons. So I'd go into Glasgow, to a man called Derek Hawkins who had played with Ted Heath, Geraldo and all the big bands. He was basically a jazz player so the things I was learning from him were jazz-oriented. I heard Charlie Parker a little later and swopped to saxophone. When I moved down to Liverpool I joined a few university groups.

> In those days Virgin Records in Bold Street used to have adverts for musicians. I'd go down there because they had cushions and headphones, and in my second-to-last year I noticed there was a band looking for a saxophone player. So I wandered over,

and on the way, it was summer [1974], there was this guy in a pith helmet, like Livingstone in Africa or something. He started talking to me: 'Oh, you're going to play with Deaf School? I'm in Deaf School. I'll take you over there.' I don't know his name to this day.

I thought, I'm a chemistry student, and he was very strange. Then he had to go off somewhere and I found an excuse not to go to the audition. I called up later and just pretended I couldn't find it. Walking towards the art college, everyone seemed really weird. I couldn't imagine myself fitting in with that.

And then in my final year the same thing happened. I was looking for a band to join and in Virgin Records there was an advert for a saxophone player. I didn't realise that it was the same band, still Deaf School. I answered the ad and this time I actually went to the audition.

When I joined there were about five Bright sisters, and Hazel Bartram was still playing the flugelhorn. Roy was on banjo and second guitar. There seemed to be people who floated in and out, that weren't exactly musicians but it was much more multi-media, almost performance art. I fitted in because I was a reasonably competent saxophone player by then, and they needed people that could play. Clive was developing as a guitarist and Steve Lindsey was always very good on the bass. Hazel was a classical musician, who would play parts, and I thought I could fill out by improvising.

Some of the most interesting stuff was coming from Max. He was writing these quirky, camp songs for Steve that were much more cabaret. Again, he's not really a trained musician, so his approach to songwriting was lateral. And they would do things that I was interested in, like a weird little Scottish jig that I used to play, and things that were more jazzy.

Deaf School was a big outfit. I didn't join because I was mates with these people, I joined because they needed somebody who could play in the way that I could. So different parts of the band always hung, different cliques. I used to hang with Max a lot, and when we were travelling I gravitated towards him. But Tim lived just around the corner, so I used to hang with him and Ziggy, his girlfriend. But for me it was never a social club. I was kind of odd in the group because I was the only one who wasn't connected with the art college. I was from a slightly different background and I always felt slightly off to one side.

I was open-minded so far as image went. I would say, What do you want me to wear? They'd find me things. I remember wearing a tailed suit jacket and shorts and hats. Kevin Ward sold me a demob suit that I used to wear, I still wear it at gigs, whereas they were generating this stuff themselves: 'Let's look this way, let's design this poster.' I was interested in music, in playing. So I allowed myself to be guided. I was making a transition.

**

Apart from Anne Martin/Bette Bright, one more legacy of the O'Connor's stint was Ken Testi, a man who became

Deaf School's staunchest ally in the many decades ahead. His appearance on the scene was a hint that Rag Week was over, so to speak. Deaf School were about to become a real band.

'Ken's an interesting character in himself,' says Enrico:

The thing I like about Ken is when we did the O'Connor's Tavern gig, we were the support band and Ken was in the headline band. I don't know what they were called but they had big leather belts with big buckles, tight trousers with their balls on show, loons and long hair, that's what they were going for. As I remember in the set they were doing 'Only the crumbliest, flakiest chocolate' [a Cadbury TV advert of the time] in this heavy rock way, and when we came on Ken was just like, that's when he quit that band. He saw it straight away. He was bright enough to say, 'Oh, my band is so wrong, I'm out of here.'

He came straight over and said, 'I wanna work with you guys.' Isn't that lovely? His band was good, they could knock us out of the ring on any of that macho posturing and rock. And we come on, big mess, with a crowd, the whole place goes mad, and Ken goes, 'Ah, I've got it, something's happening here.' And he became our sound guy.

Testi was playing bass that night, in his own band Great Day. In fact, they had already decided it would be their last gig, but it's true that he found Deaf School a revelation. 'I did at that moment nail myself to the Deaf School mast,' he confirms. 'It was a game-changer.'

Ken Testi's path to O'Connor's that evening was a strange one. A pensive, lugubrious man with sad bloodhound eyes, he is a rock'n'roll lifer who's observed the business from every angle and brought some much-needed experience into Deaf School's world. The future co-founder of Eric's Club in Liverpool, he'd grown up around the north-west, with pub-manager parents who moved so often his childhood 'was like the witness-protection programme'. And he helped, indirectly, to form one of the biggest bands in rock history, Queen.

Back in 1969, Ken was road manager for a Widnes blues-rock band called Ibex. Down in London he got to know Brian May and Roger Taylor, the guitarist and drummer of another struggling band, Smile. A third young man of their circle, Freddie Bulsara, had ambitions to be a singer, but Smile didn't need him. So Freddie joined Ibex instead. A former Ealing art student, Freddie brought glamour to Ibex straight away. On 9 September they were in Liverpool and playing a college freshers' night in the Sink, a basement club in Hardman Street. As chance would have it, Smile were in town as well that evening, so Brian and Roger dropped by.

'Brian and Roger travelled up from London with me because there was room in the van,' says Ken. 'They went for a walk round town. Returning later it emerged that they had been accosted by local youth. Dressed as Kensington's finest Roger, sensing danger, held up his college library card and informed the locals that the card confirmed that his hands were lethal weapons. The threat dispersed.'

That night they joined Freddie on stage for a jam. It was the first time these three-quarters of the eventual Queen played together in public. Within a year they were in the same band; Freddie, of course, became Freddie

Mercury. Ken Testi, meanwhile, became social secretary at St Helen's technical college, where he booked Queen to play, as well as helping the band in various capacities from tour-managing to touting their demo around record companies. (Curiously, as we shall see, Brian May was destined to cross Deaf School's path in a most significant way. And so was the old Sink club.)

Ibex soon split, but their guitarist Mike Bersin became a sound engineer in the Myrtle Street branch of the art college. By 1973 he had another band, Great Day, and Ken Testi (as a favour, he says) agreed to play bass. One day Mike mentioned a gang of kids who were rehearsing at Myrtle Street and asking for advice about gigs and equipment. Ken arranged to meet them and the O'Connor's support slot was fixed. But he was struck both by their numbers and their technical ignorance:

> I came away thinking, Right, let's just get as much hardware on site as we can, and make it up as we go along. I don't think even they knew how many were likely to be in the band. Rob Welch, a student at the college, was our sound engineer and he and I built a desk. But the show was great for us because the room was full, the art college turned up *en masse*. Given that it was Great Day's last show, we actually walked away from it in pocket, which was better than we expected.

The gear and expertise of Ken Testi and Rob Welch would serve Deaf School well. Frank Average was especially grateful, since he could now borrow a decent bass guitar. But the rest of 1974 was a time of slow preparation for the next push, dotted with shows for student audiences. Then, suddenly, just before Christmas, the band found itself *en route* to Amsterdam.

* * *

Clive had arranged some gigs at the Melkweg, a rock venue and Amsterdam's counter-cultural HQ. For the inexperienced band it was a big challenge. Their friend Kevin Ward was now doing lights for them in addition to his artwork:

> I was the lighting designer and operator. Which sounds grandiose but all I had was a box with about six lights in it and a bunch of cables, and you just hung them where you could. My big thing was moving shadows: by flicking backwards and forwards you could create amazing effects. I was always proud of my lighting. And that got me into touring with them. We got a bus and caught the ferry over. That was a huge thing for them at that stage. 'Wow, we're not just a little local band any more. We're going abroad, playing a residency in a famous club.'

Ken Testi was on hand to give logistical support:

> There were 21 people on the trip. I always describe Deaf School as my tertiary education, I was route-marched around galleries and museums for the entire week, with running commentaries by informed people. And we were given what was described as an apartment to stay in, which was amazingly big, enough for 21 sleeping bags, had a pot-bellied stove at one end and a Turk who was a caretaker. He had drugs, and when we came back from the Melkweg

he would say 'Ah, is chillum time, *ja*?' So we slept pretty well.

For each of their four nights they played with near-identical German rock bands. 'Crazy,' laughs Max Ripple. 'Absolute hippy territory.' Sandy Bright, flanked by Bette and Connie on stage, remembers an audience who lay around on cushions, and she watched a small child being given a joint by his mother. Ian Ritchie was thrilled, and regards Amsterdam as 'cementing the whole thing. I knew I wanted to be in the band. I'd never been out of the country, so the Melkweg was eye-opening for me. Chemistry students didn't do that kind of thing.'

'I know when that was,' says Bette Bright, 'because it was my 21st birthday. I think we got the booking on the premise that we were theatrical, and suddenly we had to come up with a few props and things, to try and justify our position on the bill. Then I got stranded. There was a snowstorm and everyone had gone and I ended up spending my 21st birthday stuck in Amsterdam.'

Perhaps she was fortunate. Ken Testi describes the conquerors' return to Britain as 'a pretty turbulent journey. The boat service between Harwich and the Hook of Holland was run by British Rail. We were on the *Prince George*, I believe, and quite honestly I'd have thought twice before crossing the Mersey on that. There was a storm force 10 and it was pitching so violently that a mixture of urine, vomit and blood was washing over the raised thresholds and into the corridors, it was just vile. I say blood because one old boy slipped down the stairs, they were so wet with vomit.'

Amid the bodily fluids a proper working band was being born, ready to face its breakthrough year of 1975.

A few members, like Dave Saunders and Connie Stevens, returned to college life and were not replaced, but the line-up was still ungainly at a time when rock's most revered configuration was the power trio. Bette Bright:

It was a bit wackadoo in those days. There was Nigel, in his rubber jelly suit, lit up, and sweating profusely. And there was a guy called Colin Barron: when we were down to two singers, one evening, he introduced us as the Bright Sisters, so that was how we got our name. It was all just fun. I remember once playing at an art school party, we were all miming to a Roxy song and I was on drums, and everyone kept moving around. And afterwards people were coming up and saying, 'That's amazing! I didn't know you could play so many instruments!'

✳ ✳ ✳

The making of Deaf School was a residency at the Back of the Moon, a club off Bold Street. On its Thursday rock nights it was called the Pentagon, and admission was 35 pence. Geographically, Bold Street continues downhill from Hardman Street to the heart of the city. Symbolically, the gigs represented Deaf School's transition from the student world, up on the heights of Hope Street, to the downtown bustle of actual Scouse Liverpool.

Beyond their familiar turf of college parties and O'Connor's, there were desperately few live outlets. Pubs like the Sportsman and the Moonraker, tucked inside a concrete shopping mall called St John's Precinct, offered free music by hard rock combos. But they didn't feel right, or welcoming, to Deaf School. Enrico Cadillac:

We thought, Where can we play next? Somebody in my family had just taken over the Back of the Moon. We borrowed it for rehearsals, and then we thought, Why don't make this place our own? Hey, let's do the show right here! There was already a buzz, from O'Connor's and the Sphinx Bar at the university, and we were getting a following. So I said, What if we play upstairs in your club? We'll bring our PA and all that. 'OK, no problem.'

So we started a residency, and the first gig was full. And this guy, the owner, didn't get it but he smelled an opportunity. He says, 'Why don't you do this every week, I'll give you good money' blah blah blah. And I was like, Yes, we'll do it every week but we'll give *you* a bit of money, we'll have our own guy on the door. I'll never forget turning up for the second show, the queue was right round the corner into Bold Street. And they had this horrible security guy who didn't quite get it, I had an argument with him before the show: Don't you *dare* treat these people like that.

For the third gig I went on the door myself, posing as a bouncer with my moustache and Crombie overcoat, taking the tickets before I went on stage. We did a lot of malarkey like that. Bette Bright would take the tickets, be in a little booth, no one would really notice. But eventually that club was so rammed.

And that's when Deaf School really took off. We started getting the normal kids as well as the outsider kids and art students, and maybe the gay kids who didn't quite know where to go. They all came to Deaf School. And then we got the council estate kids. What was that all about? I thought, This is really interesting. The word started to spread. Maybe it was just that they were great joyous gigs, good old rock'n'roll. But it made a bridge between the art students and maybe the more sensitive, upper echelon of the council estates.

We had real scallies at those gigs. Working-class gangs of Liverpool lads, and there's me with my moustache and eye make-up, and they're talking to me as if I haven't got it on. And Bette Bright with her posh, Whitstable Kent voice. She never changed it, and they never blinked at it.

'The Back of the Moon,' says Average, 'was a horrible, cheesy club, with strippers, but we would fill it out with our crowd, students and young people of all types.' Bette remembers the band improving dramatically, and 'then sometimes you would have people crying, not because it was dreadful but because they were so moved, I think'. According to Sandra, word even reached the pop impresario Mickie Most, who came along one night to take a look: 'We knew he was coming but it was absolutely packed and we never really saw him.'

Most, we must assume, was underwhelmed but Geoff Davies was staggered. A man who had followed the Liverpool music scene since the Beatles played the Cavern, Geoff now ran the city's hippest record shop, Probe. 'There were actually queues. This was something quite new. Live music in Liverpool had been pretty well dead since the Merseybeat days. Now it was exciting. The appeal of Deaf School started not with your average Scouser, it was more the trendies, the Hope Street end of things. But as they were seen more, and there was word of mouth, it would be Scousers as well, which says a lot. You'd get taxi drivers talking about Deaf School. They'd become massive.'

They were still an art school band in spirit (even if some members had not been to a lecture in months) and their visual presentation was streets ahead of anything else in town. Tim Whittaker, Kevin Ward and Steve Hardstaff busied themselves with posters that Ian Ritchie noticed were now appearing all over Liverpool, 'which was when I knew I was in a band that was going somewhere'. And their impact on stage cannot be understated. In a drab time of bearded, frowning virtuosi, the panache of Enrico and the sexiness of the Bright Sisters was wonderfully unusual. Ken Testi has since described them as looking like Kid Creole & the Coconuts before that band actually existed. Trouser-bottoms were being redefined by the day. As Deaf School's long-term fan Laurence Sidorczuk states: 'It was the death of the loon in Liverpool.'

The local DJ Norman Killon had followed the band from the start and marvelled at their progress:

> It was different to everything you'd been seeing at pubs like the Sportsman where bands were doing Led Zeppelin or Sabbath or whatever. Then I was working in Silly Billy's in Whitechapel at the second branch of Probe, and Steve came in. I half-recognised him, but he asked if we had Dan Hicks & His Hot Licks' album and I immediately warmed to him. Then I saw Deaf School again, when they'd decided which areas to tackle and became a much tighter ensemble. They did 'I Heard it Through the Grapevine' which very few people performed live at that point, because it was all hard rock. They were enjoying themselves.

If they were playing bum notes it didn't worry them. It was refreshing.

I regard them as the backbone of that whole scene. The great thing about Deaf School was they appealed to practically everybody who was interested in music in Liverpool. It wasn't just the bohemian section but what would generally be called the scally section. Prior to that, they had latched on to Bowie and Roxy Music, which you wouldn't expect coming from there, they'd probably get a hard time from the local hard-nuts. And I still see those kind of people wherever Deaf School play, they're there.

In the crowds that flocked to their shows that year were the young musicians – mostly not yet in bands – who would form the Second Coming of Liverpool music. Henry Priestman, Will Sergeant, Jayne Casey, Holly Johnson, Dave Balfe, Gary Dwyer, Paul Simpson, Pete Wylie, Budgie, Ian Broudie, Dave Hughes, Alan Gill and Ian McNabb were just a few. Between them they would come to populate bands such as Echo & the Bunnymen, The Teardrop Explodes, the Wild Swans, Yachts and Frankie Goes To Hollywood.

I was among the crowd of Liverpudlian fans who saw something in Deaf School that promised transformation. We neither expected or wanted a new Beatles, but we did need the Ghost of Liverpool Future. We all knew about the Ghost of Liverpool Past, it was clanking through the streets of everyone's memory. Here, suddenly, was something else. And there was remarkable unanimity on that point.

As the Bunnymen's Will Sergeant told *Record Collector*, he'd longed for art college: 'Back then, in my eyes, all the coolest hipsters went to art school.' Deaf School 'were like a breath of fresh air in a local music scene that was stagnant... They were the first post-Beatles group from Liverpool that a new generation of aspiring musicians could focus on and look up to, giving them the belief that something interesting could come out of the city. They were one of the main reasons I wanted to be in a band.'

A temporary but much-valued addition to the ranks was Mike Evans. Formerly the sax player and a main writer in Adrian Henri's Liverpool Scene, he connects Deaf School with their predecessors in the city's uptown art/pop crossover. Ian Ritchie explains how it came about:

> After about a year with Deaf School, I had my finals coming up, and I hadn't been working terribly hard. So I thought, If I'm going to get a reasonable degree out of this, I'm gonna have to knuckle down. So I basically said, I'm leaving the band, to do this. I'll contact you after I'm done and if you want me back, that's fine. And Mike Evans was a replacement for me in that period.

Evans had no formal connections to the art college – though its leading lights, from Henri and Sam Walsh to Arthur Ballard and Maurice Cockrill, were his drinking buddies – but he happened to visit one day and saw a sign on the notice board. Its gist, he says, was '"Saxophone player required, interested in rock'n'roll and Glenn Miller" or something bizarre. So I met this crazy gang, all 11 or 12 of them.'

Evans' ability was apparent and his pedigree was

impeccable. He was from Rhyl, in North Wales, and as a teenager in the 1950s had worked the fairgrounds there with a 25-year-old painter named Adrian Henri. (Henri was at that time a well-regarded artist in Liverpool 8, but like any good bohemian he always needed the cash.) By the time Mike went to college in London, he was dividing his life between the capital's emerging R&B scene and regular visits to Liverpool, which were in turn divided between Adrian's 'happenings' up in Hope Street and a rock group called the Beatles, downtown at the Cavern.

Mike Evans was thus eye-witness to two simultaneous pop revolutions. Down south he learned saxophone from Dick Heckstall-Smith, a player in the legendary Alexis Korner band that also nurtured Jack Bruce, Ginger Baker, Graham Bond, Cyril Davies, Long John Baldry and Charlie Watts. Up north he accompanied the Mersey poets in performance, and joined a second-wave Merseybeat band the Clayton Squares. From 1967 to 1970 he played in the Liverpool Scene, then moved into freelance journalism and local radio. Deaf School's advertisement caught him at an opportune moment.

Later on, for a while, he overlapped with Ian Ritchie. The saxophonist he'd stood in for scraped a 2:1 honours degree from Liverpool University and found his old band willing to bring him back. Deaf School now had a three-piece horn section of accomplished players in Mike, Ian and Hazel Bartram.

***

Nobody foresaw the next lurch into immortality, however. 'I entered the band for the *Melody Maker* Rock & Folk competition,' says Frank Average, almost apologetically. 'Which we went on and won! But I simply did that for something to do.' Run by what was then the country's leading weekly music paper, the *Melody Maker*'s annual contest was a well-established fixture on the pop calendar. Its regional heats for 1975 were held in May, with Deaf School first triumphing at Didsbury, near Manchester, and then at Leeds.

Bette Bright: 'I remember going into the rounds of that *Melody Maker* thing but it was more like a joke. The competition was all that prog rock, very odd really.' And Sam 'Eric Shark' Davis:

> For the first *Melody Maker* heat we went over to Manchester and Clive had his yellow Morris 1000 van, Ian had a Beetle and we all crammed in, bodies everywhere. We went in our stage make-up, all dressed up, and went to the bar and everyone else was in black leather and tight pants and cowboy boots, looking at us: 'What are these lot? Where did *they* come from?' I think it was because we were so different and fresh – we certainly weren't as good musicians as the others – that we won.

Max adds: 'Some people have enormous certainty about themselves, "We're gonna win" and all that stuff. But we just went through this whole rollercoaster of gathering support. It was the support as much as anything that was so amazing.' Of their early competitors, he remembers quizzing the oddly titled GYGAFO. 'Oh, that's a strange name, I said. How did you get it? They said, "It was from our first manager, we did an audition for him and he said, Get Your Gear And Fuck Off."'

And Ian Ritchie:

> We were playing one of those heats, started a tune,
> someone came in in the wrong key and the band
> were out of time. We got half-way through the
> first verse and Enrico went, 'OK, just stop. This is
> ridiculous, let's do it properly.' So we started again
> and we did it. And we won that heat. And in the
> judges' notes was, 'Great theatrical touch when the
> lead singer stopped the band.' It was just us screwing
> up, but it was perceived as being theatre.
>
> At that time there were comedy bands like
> Supercharge, Alberto Y Lost Trios Paranoias and the
> Bonzos, but Deaf School were something else. We
> did have songs, and they weren't comedy songs, but
> there was something very attractive about them and
> tongue-in-cheek, and that's what got us through.

The final was held on 28 June at the Roundhouse, a
converted railway building near Euston, which had
become a landmark rock venue in the 1960s. Previewing
the event in that week's issue, *Melody Maker* announced
that last year's winners, a progressive rock band called
Druid, were about to release their debut album *Toward
The Sun*. (Looking back, in the light of Druid's obscurity,
this was not an encouraging precedent.) Photographs of
1975's contenders show massed ranks of hair and denim,
with Deaf School a spectacular exception.

The band arrived by coach from Liverpool, with a
mob of supporters, while another contingent of friends
came up from Kent. Dave Sargeant, of the latter group,
estimates Deaf School fans formed 80 per cent of the
audience. Hazel Bartram noticed that their girl fans were

more colourful than everyone else put together. As Ian Ritchie adds: 'There were folk-rock bands, out of the Lindisfarne mould. We were odd. We've always been out of our time. We were odd in the '70s because we weren't doing 20-minute blues jams in E, and we were odd later on because we weren't really a punk band.'

'A girl in Fashion & Textiles did the dresses for Anne and me,' says Sandra. 'Anne's Mum had been on the stage and in Anne's flat in Liverpool she had a rail of her Mum's old clothes. Before we did a gig we'd get things from there, and I'd buy second-hand clothes as well. But for the Roundhouse I had this black plastic dress with windows in it, and silhouettes of people in the windows, Anne's was printed with records and music notes, a 1950s look. We had bright fluorescent underskirts.'

There were 13 bands competing that night, plus four solo acts in a separate category. Deaf School were positioned late in the bill, which Ken Testi took as a favourable omen. His spirits were further raised when he found that one of the judges was his old friend Brian May. 'Ken! What are you doing here?' asked the curly-maned guitarist. 'I'm with one of the bands,' he replied.

'Don't tell me which one.'

'I wouldn't dream of it, Brian. But you'll know.'

It was reasonable to hope a member of Queen would recognise and reward some good old-fashioned theatricality.

May's fellow judges were *Melody Maker*'s editor Ray Coleman, the *Old Grey Whistle Test* presenter Bob Harris, a Persian folk singer and recent *Maker* discovery called Shusha, and two EMI executives Nick Mobbs and Martin Clarke. On their score sheets they were to award a total of 100 points, of which 70 were for 'musical ability' and 30 for 'presentation'. One might have wished, for Deaf School's sake, that it were the other way around.

And yet they won. Full marks for presentation and 60 out of 70 for ability. 'Tremendous stuff,' the judges decreed. 'Britain's answer to Sha Na Na!' Beating off the runners-up, who included a Status Quo-like band from Rotherham called Hot Property, they were to collect prize money of £1000, half in cash and half in vouchers for musical instruments.

The Roundhouse erupted, and not only Deaf School's own vociferous contingent. Sandy Bright ran to the stage and collided with Bob Harris as she did so. Ian Ritchie was frankly amazed:

> I'd had one big solo and just before I was supposed to play it, my saxophone strap broke. A tenor is too heavy to hold and move all your fingers around. You couldn't actually play it. So I went to the front of the stage, pulled Enrico's microphone right down and got on one knee, put the saxophone on the ground and played it like that. Again, in one of the judges' notes it was 'Great theatrical touch when the saxophone player did that.' It was only because of some silly mistake.

Their tutor and former band-member Dave Saunders was looking on with pride: 'Until we went to the Roundhouse and won the *Melody Maker* contest, I'd always thought of them as part of the experimental music scene, rather than pop music. But I remember thinking they'd won this hands down. I went to the bar and lined up all the drinks. It was an amazing night and I couldn't believe I was part of all this.'

The front page of the following week's *Melody Maker*, dated 5 July, displayed Deaf School in all their triumph. 'I've still got it,' says Average. 'It's like looking at the Kop, it's just a sea of faces all smiling cos we'd won.' The impact of the celebrating throng is a little diminished by the inclusion of a stranger, foreground and centre, sandwiched between Bette and Sandy. (He was, in fact, Ivan Chandler, a pianist and winner of the solo artist section; his own eventual career would be more in music publishing than performance.) Back at the Roundhouse, Deaf School wondered if life could ever get better than this.

'We were absolutely elated that we won,' says Sandra, 'we took it by storm. I remember us all coming back on the coach and obviously drinking quite a lot. We didn't stay the night, we went there and back in a day. It was all so exciting, even the heats. And after that, people got interested.' Much of the prize money, though, had to go on replacing Ian Ritchie's instrument: 'I lost my saxophone,' he says. 'When it was announced that we'd won, I was actually down on the floor space with a bunch of friends. As it was a group of people I didn't say to one person, "Please look after my saxophone while I go onstage." I said it to the group. And obviously everybody thought somebody else would do it. I went on stage, they wandered off and I never saw the saxophone again. I got extremely drunk and was extremely ill on the bus back to Liverpool.'

Bette Bright corroborates this: 'My overriding memory is that after we'd won it we were driving back on a coach to Liverpool, triumphant, and we stopped on the Finchley Road. Clive's dad's friend had a restaurant there and we got a case of wine. So we were shooting along merrily up the motorway and all of a sudden, Ian Ritchie, who was behind me, did this huge projectile vomit of red wine all over me. Like a fountain. Oh my God. We stopped at the services. This sound-guy's girlfriend, a real hippy, fortunately she had a change of clothing. So I came back in hippy cheesecloth.'

Vomit and lost saxophones notwithstanding, they all remember this night as a turning point in their fortunes. But it was a strangely ambiguous victory. As Max Ripple says, 'It was one of the great moments of my life. Just sitting in the Roundhouse, with the tumultuous sound of the response to our winning. It was like half of Liverpool was there. "My God, I'll never have this moment again." It was an incredible pleasure and delight to reach that high pinnacle. Which was of course the kiss of death in terms of being taken seriously.'

Bette Bright: 'It was good to have won it, but then people were going, it was like the kiss of death, whoever wins that. It was double edged.' Max again: 'The *Melody Maker* thing galvanised a lot of interest around us, as well as in the band. Winning it certainly surprised *me*. So on the one hand we got lots of record company interest, but at the same time some disparaging comments in the press. You kind of felt it's not really cool to win the *Melody Maker* competition.'

There's something in this theory. For all *Melody Maker*'s prestige at that time, talent contests were redolent of old-fashioned show business, of 1950s holiday camps and tacky TV shows like Hughie Green's *Opportunity Knocks*. They were antithetical to a rock sensibility that prized 'paying your dues', building your art and your fan-base organically. (The same scepticism attaches itself to twenty-first-century talent shows such as *The X Factor*.) By 1980 the Rock and Folk contest had been re-jigged as a Battle of the Bands competition, and soon disappeared entirely. Needless to say, *Melody Maker*'s pugnacious weekly rivals, *Sounds* and the *NME*, automatically scorned the darlings of another newspaper. All three papers had huge influence back then, but their internecine war was vicious. An unintended consequence was that Deaf School were caught in the crossfire.

More romantically, the journey home to Liverpool marked a new stage in the blossoming offstage story of Bette and Enrico. Steve Allen says of Anne Martin:

> I fell head over heels for her. Like nothing I'd ever known. I don't know if that was because she was posh totty, though that was attractive. But she was with Kevin [Ward], who was a bit of a god, with his great hair like David Bowie, a very athletic guy. So I didn't think anything would come of it. But I did become a bit besotted. If we were in the Grapes and Anne came in, the room lit up. I wasn't going to try and pull her, but I was nuts about her.
>
> Anne sat next to me on the coach coming back from the *Melody Maker* and asked if she could put her head in my lap to have a sleep. That was our little bonding thing. That was the beginning of it. And I wrote a few lyrics in that time, like 'A Bigger Splash'. And it was autumn, a time heavy with atmosphere, especially in Liverpool around Princes Road, with all those trees.
>
> When we became an item we moved into a flat in Catharine Street. Very cosy. Clive was a bit left out because of it. And we were still together through the

second and third albums. It was awkward, initially. It was difficult for Clive because it was hard to get me. I was a bit too happy to write anything.

***

Record companies were now pursuing Deaf School, and it was time to put the whole art school prank on a business footing. Enter a young man named Frank Silver, a friend of Clive's. 'I was in a band with him at school,' says the guitarist, 'he was the keyboard player. When he left school he went straight to working at the Roundhouse and became house manager there, and always studied economics and was money conscious. So when we were thinking about managers he came to mind, even though he hadn't done it before. He's tough with money and understood music to a certain extent. I don't know if he understood Deaf School, he was more of an ELP kind of guy. But at that time he fitted the bill.'

Frank Silver himself:

Clive and I had grown up together in Hampstead, very good friends, we'd been in a band with Julien Temple. Clive went off to Liverpool and I went into music merchandising, then I worked at the Roundhouse where I was exposed to the music business, its characters and stories. And the conclusion both Clive and I had was that the music business was dangerous, there were people who would rip you off at the drop of a hat.

When Deaf School won the *Melody Maker* contest at the Roundhouse, I was there in my professional capacity as assistant house manager, after cleaning toilets and tearing tickets and bouncing on the door. I was quite a business-like young man, a straight, disciplined guy and not a party animal like everyone seemed to be. All of a sudden record companies were clamouring to sign Deaf School, Clive asked me to help. Whilst I was inexperienced, I was a trusted pair of hands, trusted to execute Clive's wishes, I wasn't rapacious.

Clive and I had come from comfortable backgrounds and we weren't fazed by money. We were sophisticated young men. My role became to play the field with the record companies. I assumed, with Clive, that they would be as successful as the Beatles. We didn't expect failure and we needed proper advice from accountants and solicitors. I was determined on Clive's behalf not to get ripped off. We set up a corporate structure, with a telling name: Deaf School formed a limited company to act as a vehicle to collect their monies, called Shark Music Ltd, because they thought the world was infested by sharks, and this was their defence.

My company, Swingbest Ltd, was formed to act as their production vehicle. I would retain the rights and lease them to the record companies, to protect the group and its huge wealth when they hit the jackpot.

As Clive recalls of Frank: 'He took it very seriously, and made money for himself, but we never really cared about the money at that time. He was a bit unpopular with some of the people in the band, but I think they appreciated the fact that he took the business seriously. Nobody else had any knowledge of how to deal with that world. And it was good for me because he was an old friend and I could talk to him. But a lot of the band were happy to let someone take responsibility and get on with it.'

The initial interest that followed the *Melody Maker* win turned into a bidding contest. Virgin led the field: 'We were wooed by Richard Branson,' says Clive. 'Steve and I especially, going to the Manor [Branson's converted country house in Oxfordshire] and having a smoke with him. And Rocket [an Elton John-owned record label] were kind of interested. And Richard Williams, who was Island's A&R and looking after Roxy Music, was interested.' And EMI, the biggest British label of all, had a relationship with the *Melody Maker* contest that gave them automatic rights to at least audition the winners. But at the same time, there was also Warner Brothers.

Warner Brothers! Burbank, California! The home of Bugs Bunny!

FOUR

Bunny Money

How to Upset Richard Branson – The
Yankee Dollar – 2nd Honeymoon

EMI WERE RULED OUT early on. Sandy Bright remembers
that 'somebody there asked would I not like to go solo,
cos I had a very loud voice and would I not like to be the
next Cilla Black? I said you've got to be joking!' Island
Records, for all its hip prestige, was likewise dismissed. In
Frank and Clive's view, this had become a two-horse race
between Virgin and Warner Brothers. In more personal
terms, it was a choice between two men, Richard Branson
and Derek Taylor.

Both suitors had formidable reputations. Virgin's
founder was just becoming known to mainstream Britain
as the brash, bearded hippy capitalist who turned business
conventions upside down. Warners' man was the pop

world's equivalent of an old-fashioned gentleman, the diplomatic and softly spoken Northerner who had handled the Beatles' PR through the best and the worst of times. It seemed a case of unstoppable ambition versus cultivated charm.

According to their tyro manager, Frank Silver: 'We were young, I was 21, completely naive, but I played poker and was good at keeping a straight face. I trotted round record companies, with Clive and Steve if there were artistic discussions but usually on my own for the business ones. It basically turned into a bidding war between Virgin and Warners and it just became a job of trying to up the ante.'

In 1975 Rob Dickins was the young MD of Warner Brothers' UK publishing company. Like a lot of people, his eye was caught by Deaf School's *Melody Maker* coverage:

> So I went to see them at UCL in Bloomsbury. I fell in love with them, thought they were fantastic, went backstage and met them. They had a manager but didn't know much about anything, and they were being wooed by a few people, but not publishers. I was about 26, but most publishers were 40 back in those days, so they weren't at gigs like that. I went to the record company and said to Derek Taylor, You've got to sign this band.
>
> We were in the era of pub rock, when you had Dr Feelgood, and you had the progressives, and suddenly you had this band that was so refreshing when you went out to gigs every night, with elements of Roxy Music, the Beatles, the Bonzo Dog Band, and very much the art college band. They all had different names, before it happened in punk times. With the costumes, the images, they were very refreshing

against a tedious backdrop of one-dimensional music at the time.

In fact one of Derek Taylor's Warner scouts, Pete Swettenham, had already seen Deaf School at the Roundhouse and approached them that very night. (Pete was a former member of Grapefruit, a band signed to the Beatles' Apple label when Derek was running its PR side. He would later go on to engineer for Deaf School.) Between these recommendations from two such trusted sources, Derek took a trip up north to watch this band in its native habitat. It probably helped that Liverpool was his home town.

It helped even more that he saw the band rehearse in O'Halligan's. This building (of which more later) was a new hub of alternative culture in Liverpool, comprising market stalls, a café and performance space that the band were now using regularly. Symbolically, it was in Mathew Street, just a few doors down from the site of the old Cavern Club. 'He was quite emotional,' remembers Clive, 'because it was Liverpool and he just thought, "Wow, it was all happening again."' Enrico picks up the story:

> We couldn't resist Derek Taylor. That was the problem. The romance was too strong, and his eloquence. If you fall in love with Derek Taylor, what are you gonna do? We were talking to Richard Branson, when Derek comes up to see us in O'Halligan's. It was just a big warehouse but we were well-established in our set-up there, sounded good. And, Derek pulled up a chair in front of us and started crying.
>
> It was amazing. We did 'Get Set Ready Go', we did

'Room Service', we did something else, and when we looked up there were tears running down his cheeks. And that was it. You're not gonna sign to someone like that? No contest. We stopped rehearsing and went over and said, 'Is everything OK?' He said 'Don't stop playing this wonderful music. I'm here, this is where it all began, in Mathew Street, with another new band I'm excited by.'

I think he loved Deaf School because he could see elements of other things he liked, not the Beatles, but cabaret, Noel Coward, Oscar Wilde, John Betjeman's poetry. Anne fell in love with Derek completely.

Clive adds: 'We were still keen on Virgin. But Derek came in offering us 12 per cent and signing to America with a production deal, an amazing deal. Virgin were offering 8 per cent, which was rubbish really, but they loved us.' Apart from Derek's warmth and generosity, thinks Rob Dickins, there was also the charisma of the American label: 'the whole idea of Warner Brothers, the logo, Hollywood. That captivated them.'

Frank Silver saw it was time to wrap up negotiations: 'Derek Taylor, who is one of the most marvellous men I've had the pleasure to meet, fell in love with the group. Being a Liverpool man himself he understood them. And because of his Beatle experience, he believed they would be the next big thing. So whatever Virgin offered, I was able to go to Derek and say, You'll have to do better. This went on for a number of weeks, and while I was waiting for a new draft contract from Virgin, Warner Brothers came in with an amazing offer. So we agreed terms and that was that.'

Unfortunately, that was not *entirely* that. In early

September the band were booked to play at the Nashville, a pub venue in West London. 'Richard Branson turned up to sign the band,' says Frank. 'Which was very rock'n'roll and funny. It was Clive who told him, "Actually, we've signed with Warner Brothers." Richard Branson went mad.' As Clive recalls: 'He walked out. Then I had to go onstage and I was freaked out completely. It had upset me.'

Enrico Cadillac Jnr:

> Richard Branson was coming to our gigs with a top hat on and a moustache and everything. You know what he's like. A top hat like an undertaker. He was absolutely convinced Deaf School were signing to him, our manager never told Richard that we'd signed to Warners, and we thought he'd let them know. And we'd been out to the Manor, Branson had invited me and Clive, we were playing snooker with him, so we felt pretty bad.

Not as bad as Branson, though. A legendarily competitive man, he made his displeasure clear to Frank Silver and there followed a long correspondence before the Warner deal was cleared. Clive Langer, who has had three decades to reflect upon their eventual choice, says, 'It would have been a different story had we signed to them. Maybe we could have got the credibility that we had in Liverpool. I liked being with the Virgin people, I could relate to them better, but Derek was an incredible figure, I loved him more. I don't think we made a wrong decision. And we wouldn't have gone to America.'

***

So who was Derek Taylor, and why was he so wonderful?

Liverpool-born, raised on the Wirral, Taylor became a journalist and progressed from the *Hoylake Advertiser* to the showbiz desk of the *Daily Express*. Having covered the start of Beatlemania he became the group's PR in 1964, and in the same year penned some characteristic sleevenotes for their LP *Beatles for Sale* ('When, in a generation or so, a radio-active, cigar-smoking child, picknicking on Saturn, asks you what the Beatles affair was all about...'). He ghost-wrote their manager Brian Epstein's elegant autobiography *A Cellarful of Noise*.

At the dawn of hippydom he moved to Los Angeles and was pressman-cum-*consigliere* to the Beach Boys, the Byrds, Captain Beefheart, the Mamas & the Papas and more, as well as instigating 1967's historic Monterey Festival. He returned to England to resume PR for the Beatles in their late, troubled phase at Apple, which included helping John and Yoko through their peace campaigning. He was loved by journalists for his calm eloquence and ever-open drinks cabinet, but in the process became an alcoholic and a heavy user of LSD. Taylor was a dreamy, middle-class Scouse idealist who understood hard-bitten Fleet Street hacks.

He stayed at Apple beyond the Beatles' bitter falling out. I interviewed him in 1988, when he told me: 'I was looking after the dying embers. But I never accepted the break-up. The Beatles will never break up, they won't get back together, they can't now, but they will never be ex-Beatles.' In 1971, with his reputation at its zenith, he moved to Warner Brothers' London office as MD, prior to its absorption into the newly created WEA (short for Warner-Elektra-Atlantic).

These were high times in the music industry and Derek had a pretty free hand, his first signing being Liverpool jazzer George Melly, whose campaign throws light on his later dealings with Deaf School. Derek told me:

It was big spending and big boozing: 'Mellymania'. And it worked because he was so wonderful. I was never afraid to take on people who wouldn't make it into the charts. I never saw the charts as the real measure of value. I never felt wounded if my albums didn't sell. I never took it personally.

And the back-up from the American company was fabulous. Things were lavish. There was an enormous amount of money being thrown about. WEA didn't make money, it lost, but that wasn't the point. We had all that money because, as a result of Monterey, the record business had discovered a new market for that other kind of music. So they were feeling their way and throwing a lot of money at it.

And because England still had a certain cachet, you had to do well in London. The American companies were happy to take a bit of a loss in England so long as we showed their acts a good time. And that meant lunching, parties, receptions, meeting them at the airport with enormous limousines and people with flowers. I used to bring them back from Heathrow by the Windsor route instead of that awful Hogarth Roundabout way, try and bring them in the beautiful way. It was always trying to show people a good time, that was the thing.

His PR philosophy stayed with him now he was a company executive. 'Artists are reachable,' he told me, 'and so deeply human and insecure, that if you can slot into that – the fact that we're all fucked up, we're little children, weak, we're all in this struggle to get by as best we can – then you can be a publicist and you can be their friend.' As well as George Melly his Scouse signings included Scaffold and Liverpool Express, acts rooted in Hope Street and Mathew Street respectively.

Was money wasted, I wondered? 'Well, what is money wasted?' he replied. 'It depends what you think money is for. I've always felt it was for spreading about. And if that means giving Sparks some leather overcoats to get them through an English winter then that's OK, especially as the coats would be made by some hippy pixies we knew.'

He swore off drink in 1975 and found Deaf School the same year. It was a mutual love affair that never went sour. Bette Bright: 'Derek Taylor was always nice. Like, when you got the Christmas hamper, he'd get us an extra three so we weren't going to starve in Liverpool. Then he'd give us the account number so I could always get a cab in London. He was fabulous, old Derek. Then I guess we started recording and he was around. One of the first things I did at Air Studios, Steve had had a wig-out and stomped off, and it was, "Oh you might as well do 'Final Act'. Oh God." But he was there and he was great, really supportive and calm. I remember that.'

Clive Langer: 'Derek was a hippy, a dreamer like John Lennon, and he took a lot of acid with them. But he still had his cravat: Derek's leaning towards hippy-ness was that he wore a scarf around his neck when the Beatles were doing *Sgt. Pepper*. Derek was fantastic for Deaf School, he was a very important part of believing in ourselves and giving us confidence. And listening. I loved him.'

And so they signed to the beguiling Mr Taylor, in the teeth of Richard Branson's opposition. On Monday, 1 December 1975, a coach-load of Warner employees were brought to the Everyman Theatre in Hope Street for an invitation-only showcase for the new act. 'The initial deal, as I remember,' says Frank Silver, 'was £45,000, which sounds like nothing now but was a lot of money then. And there were additional sums. I was constantly going to them for another 15,000. By the time Warners finished, their investment in the group must have been, conservatively, 150 grand. Which was very significant in those days.'

Melody Maker, still taking a paternal interest in its protégés, devoted column inches to a Derek Taylor announcement: 'I haven't felt the same about a band since I first saw the Byrds ten years ago.' He called the new arrangement 'a very hard, expensive deal... They're a hell of a signing. I don't see anything to stop them becoming huge and popular. Their songs are excellent and their attitude is happy and intelligent.' Voluptuous and expensive pages of advertising would follow. As Frank Silver says:

> We were treated very well by Warner Brothers, spoiled, in fact. The deal was a production deal, we didn't want artistic control to go to a record label. So we said to Warners, Yes, you can market the records but you're only licensing them, you don't have the soul of the group. And my company Swingbest retained the rights but I had to account to the band's company, Shark. So we thought we'd set up a very

intelligent structure to deal with the massive success that was going to flow to us over the next few years.

The royalties we obtained from Warners were extremely good, 12, 13, 14 per cent which in those days were top flight. And we were very well-funded, they had three albums guaranteed: 'We're going to sign you, we're going to grow you, spend the money, develop you.' There was no hesitation from Warners about money, because it was Derek's baby. Derek was highly thought of within Warners, a charming, clever man. Derek had persuaded Mo Ostin who was the head of Warners, in Burbank. He sold the band, internally.

Mo used to complain to Derek that I was always asking him for more money. But I had eight mouths to feed every week. It was an expensive operation. Not that they got paid a lot of money but if you add up the bills, eight people in a hotel is quite an overhead on tour, and you can't transport eight people in the back of a car. The sheer size of the group was a cost. And Warners, bless them, coughed up.

Duly signed, the team was obliged to consolidate: there were no more guest members performing whimsical walk-on roles.

✷✷✷

One of the best musicians, Hazel Bartram, had already left. Much as she had enjoyed the *Melody Maker* win, she foresaw it taking Deaf School into a new world. With heavy heart, she says, she resigned to concentrate on her studies and complete her course. This she did, graduating successfully and moving on to a lifetime's career in music and the visual arts. (She had also been drawn into the orbit of the Portsmouth Sinfonia, performing at the Albert Hall and playing on their 1979 album *20 Classic Rock Classics*.) In 1995 she married and, as Hazel Bartram-Birchenough, moved to the USA. Today she runs a studio in Houston, exhibits widely and works and tours with various choirs. 'They had good antennae in Deaf School,' she smiles. 'Everyone went on to have some form of success. They didn't pick people who wouldn't.'

Then Mike Evans resigned. Well-versed in the music business, he knew that Derek wished the band were smaller. He had his personal reasons, too:

> I left voluntarily after the *Melody Maker* thing because I literally didn't want to go on the road again. It had been great fun as an amateur band, but I'd had enough of the heavy duty rock'n'roll lifestyle. I'd done the Clayton Squares and Liverpool Scene, done the American thing, lost money, slept in vans, all the romantic stuff that isn't romantic when you do it. I was enjoying doing local radio and being the *Melody Maker's* man in Liverpool, and I had two kids by then. The band were quite shocked, but I thought it was time to leave.

The band look back on Evans' tenure with gratitude. Steve 'Average' Lindsey says, 'He was a big influence. Deaf School always did a few covers and he brought ideas along with him. There was a song called "It Should Have Been Me", which I think was made famous by Ray Charles; we used to do "Blueberry Hill" as well. But he was around for a good period of time while the Deaf School sound was being honed.' According to Mike himself, 'Clive said to me later, "You taught us how to do it. The way you went about pinning down the arrangements, nothing too fancy." I was a bit of an editor, because it was a big outfit, and without some editing it could have been a shambles.' Evans went on to a busy career as musician, author and broadcaster, and for several years was a national organiser for the Musicians Union.

His departure, and Hazel's, left Ian Ritchie as the sole survivor of the horn section. On graduation from the university, Ian had to consider a 'proper' job offer, from a laboratory in Macclesfield:

I had a discussion with my dad [himself a scientist] about whether I should stay on with this band, or should I take up this job? I expected him to go, 'Take the job, you've just spent three years in college doing all this work.' And he surprised the hell out of me. He plays accordion, the worst accordion player on the planet, and he said, 'If I'd had the opportunity to play the accordion in a Scottish dance band, I would have done it. I did this other thing because I didn't have that opportunity.' For him, I had fulfilled my part of the bargain by getting a degree, it gave me something to fall back on.

When Deaf School signed to Warner Brothers, it only took me a month or so to really know that I was going to be a musician, not a chemist. I had no concept that you could do something you enjoyed so much and make money out of it. As soon as I had any inkling of being a musician there was no going back.

Between signing and recording, the band's shrinking line-up was profiled by a small 'Official Fan Club book' of early 1976. Self-produced, it presents poignant snapshots of a band on the brink. Enrico, we learn, has a penchant for sports cars and 'moody moments lazing after a picnic'. Frank Average Esq. likes 'economical bass' and illustrates himself with a semi-detached house. 'Timothy John Whittaker' cites a respected local drummer Ron Parry, as well as Charlie Watts, plus AquaTec Paints. 'Roy B Hold', guitarist, likes 'early English dance bands: Savoy Orpheans, Savoy Havana Dance Band, etc.'

Sandy Bright is both a 'songstress' and 'the world's best saxophonist', who likes 'Roy's spaghetti bolognaise' as well as Crimplene dresses. Bette Bright, on the other hand, is a 'chanteuse' but looks coldly on Nylon sheets and bluebottles. Eric Shark loves his wife and kids and caps from the Liverpool department store Blacklers, but not bad art and cheap shoes. 'Cliff Hanger' likes recording studios, the painter Morris Louis and *West Side Story*. He hates 'trouble'. Ian Ritchie, drawn in a tartan cap, approves of Scotch whisky, Scottish birds, Scots musicians, Scott of the Sahara and The Great McGonigle. But he hates Andy Stewart.

Finally, and more obscurely, the Very Reverend Max Ripple self-describes as 'Crusader/Philosopher/Crashing Bore/Keyboards but loves Daddies Sauce, The true mystical essence of Mankind's anthropological legacy and finally Pear-shaped tits.' Well, it takes all sorts.

***

There are Warner press ads for Deaf School showing two Bright Sisters and Roy Holt in the line-up, but neither

Roy nor Sandra actually got as far as signing record contracts. Deaf School, she says, 'had meetings and they didn't want Roy to continue in the band. They didn't like his guitar playing which was more blues and jazz based, they wanted something more rock. He played banjo in the band as well.' This accords roughly with Clive's recollection. Of the many who left Deaf School along the way, Roy was perhaps the only member who was formally sacked. By and large, says Clive, the attrition was natural:

> Losing some people wasn't too serious because *they* weren't very serious. By the time things were moving there were nine of us, but I had to ask Roy to leave. He played the banjo, and when he played electric guitar I wanted more power, and he was just meek, really. A very nice guy but his guitar playing wasn't that strong. His part of the band was the Essoldo Cinema Orchestra bit, a ragtime band. I didn't want a ragtime band, I wanted a serious rocking outfit.
>
> So he left. We thought we could talk Sandra into staying, but she was going out with him, and she said No. She was attractive and a good singer. So to get rid of her was a bit of a shock for Warner Brothers but it had to be done, and that's when Anne flourished. Before, it was quite light-hearted: it wasn't embarrassing if you saw those people at your gigs. But with Roy it was a big deal. But I had to do what I thought, whether it was right or wrong.

Average comments, 'As we got more serious, peripheral people fell away. It was a pretty loose thing, so I don't recall anyone ever being pushed. It would kind of be "Oh,

we're not doing the Essoldo Cinema Orchestra this week."
"Oh, OK, fair enough. See you at the gig anyway."'

'It became difficult for me to stay,' confirms Sandra,
'because Roy left. We were close, we got married
afterwards.' She received a letter from Derek Taylor asking
her to stay: 'But I left because I was in love with this bloke
at this time. And it was a big mistake because it was great
fun, and they did a lot after I left. At the same time, I was
now spending more time singing than painting, which
is what I was supposed to be at art college to do.' As
for Roy, she thinks, 'It was probably a bit hurtful, rather
than a shock. But he had other things going on, he was
much more into his painting. I didn't think Roy was very
bothered, really. I maybe wished *I'd* carried on, but I had
no hard feelings towards them.'

Sandra Harris went on to get a 2:1 honours degree and
marry Roy Holt, though they eventually divorced. She
moved from abstract painting into antique dealing and
now has her own interior design business in Chester. Roy
transferred to London to study and teach at Goldsmiths
before returning to Liverpool to resume in the Fine Art
department. According to Bryan Biggs, 'he continued his
art practice and was relatively successful. He carried on
making art until he died.' Roy and Sandra met again, by
chance, at Deaf School's 2006 reunion at the Picket. He
died, shortly afterwards, of cancer.

In the *Liverpool Echo* of 29 April 1976, there appeared
a story headlined POP GROUP IS SEEKING A 'CRAZY'
GIRL WITH A FIGURE. The tireless Ken Testi, billed as
said band's 'logistics expert', explained that Sandy Bright
had left Deaf School ('Liverpool's top pop group') because
the touring schedule was too heavy. 'Now we need to find

a replacement to join Bette Bright, the other singing sister. She will have to be completely out of her mind, crazy, look good, have a nice figure, sing in tune and be willing to tour.' The item goes on to describe a £45,000 contract with Warners, under ex-Beatle aide Derek Taylor, and states they are now recording *2nd Honeymoon* in London.

As Bette Bright recalls:

> Just before we started recording Clive had booted Roy out of the band and Sandra left because they were together. Then we made attempts to find another Bright Sister but it was really difficult. I remember having auditions. And funnily enough, Judy Tzuke came for an audition. She was very nice and we got on well but it wasn't right for her. [Tzuke soon launched a solo career and became famous for her 1979 hit 'Stay With Me Till Dawn'.] We often used to play with Darts, and Rita, the black girl singer, her name was Martin, which was the same as mine. So I said it should be the Martin Sisters because, you know, 'What the hell happened there?' Anyway, Bright Sister came there none. And that was that.

Early fans of the band would find it strange to suddenly see a Bright Sister in the singular. But there was soon no doubt that Anne Martin, of Whitstable, had deep reserves of glamour, soul and stage presence.

Clive and Steve/Enrico, meanwhile, showed their own commitment to Deaf School's future by dropping out of art school. 'We tried to put Deaf School in as course work,' pleads Steve. 'But it was a last-ditch effort. We were trying it on, because we were putting more time into Deaf School than into our work. And that's one of the reasons it stayed so performance art, because that side of it made sense in trying to get it accepted as our art work. Anyway, they didn't accept it and we never did our final years.'

Where Steve was expelled for sheer non-attendance, Clive actually resigned: 'I remember going to the Principal, and him telling me I was making a terrible mistake by going into music. We'd signed to Warner Brothers by then, I think I had two terms left but I hadn't actually done any work for a year. So I said, Could the band not be the piece? I could have given them this record and said, Here it is mate, here's the thesis. But they weren't having it.'

Slimming down as they were, Clive knew the band needed a boost of rock energy: 'We were signed to Warners, so we were quite a big thing already. Who plays guitar really well? The whole ethic of not being able to play had changed by then. It was "How can we compete with Roxy Music? How can we sound really good?"' In the quest for extra firepower he turned to a musician called Paul Pilnick. 'He just turned up. He was a bit rockist, and a lot older. But we liked him and he was powerful with his Telecaster and he was what we wanted.'

Pilnick in fact had more experience than the rest of the band put together. He was a Liverpudlian veteran of the Merseybeat scene who had played at the Cavern, his bands including the All-Stars and the Big Three. He'd backed the Beatles' old employer Tony Sheridan, played sessions for the Apple label, and joined Gerry Rafferty's band Stealers Wheel for their early 1970s hits including 'Stuck in the Middle with You'. For a while his career took him to America:

But I came back very disillusioned. I'd been playing a lot in the American genre and felt I hadn't moved on, it wasn't me. Despondency had set in from the overuse of a certain white substance, so I gave up playing and started listening to all types of music that had nothing to do with what I'd been doing, such as Jacques Brel. And that's when Deaf School arrived to save my life in music.

I remember thinking, Wow, what a great band. Raw, slightly amateurish, but everyone had a great idea of what they were doing. I recognised where Langer the Clanger was coming from. I'd worked with Johnny Kidd & the Pirates in Hamburg and loved Mick Green's Telecaster approach, and Clive understood Telecaster language. When the other guitarist left I put myself forward, convinced I could bring some experience and ideas to the band, and it worked out well.

* * *

So now there was an album to be made. Their appointed producer was to be Muff Winwood, once a well-regarded musician in the Spencer Davis Group (although out-shone by his brilliant younger brother Steve) and latterly the studio overseer for Sparks' breakthrough LP *Kimono My House*. Derek Taylor negotiated Winwood's fee, and with a typical flourish insisted it be upgraded to guineas rather than pounds.

The young band had made a few studio trips for demo purposes but were far from savvy. They had recorded at EMI's office in Manchester Square as part of their

Melody Maker reward, and at 10cc's Strawberry Studios in Stockport. There was another demo session at Amazon, in Liverpool, though Tim Whittaker couldn't make it. They recorded without drums anyway, and sent the results to Island among others.

The first encounter with Muff Winwood was not auspicious. Having honed their repertoire in live shows and rehearsals, Deaf School assumed they were ready to go. 'I remember some very traumatic pre-recording things,' says Ian Ritchie. 'It was a basement club in Finchley Road and we were basically routining tunes like "A Bigger Splash" and "Snapshots", those core songs for the first album. Muff started to rearrange them; we'd never experienced somebody going, "We'll go to the chorus there," or, "Leave this bit out, we don't need it." There was a lot of friction, because *we* thought the songs were perfect. We were very attached to the way we did them. And it was upsetting to have Muff disassemble and reassemble them.'

Proper recording began at Basing Street Studios in Notting Hill – owned by Island but often used by companies such as Warners – in late April 1976. Things did not go smoothly. According to Frank Silver, 'The difficulty of getting on to a tape something that they heard in their heads was very frustrating. The difficulty of producing a record... Muff I think did a very competent job but it wasn't quite how the group wanted it to be. But I'm not sure they ever made the record they heard in their heads.'

Over the next fortnight they taped the basic tracks of four songs: 'What a Way to End it All', 'Knock Knock Knocking', 'Room Service' and 'Hi Jo Hi'. There was also an unused Eric Shark/Sam Davis song, 'Play it Again, Sam'.

('A great track,' says Enrico, 'with a big Hammond organ. A bit corny but at that time we were playing with corny.') But after that, Deaf School and Muff Winwood went their separate ways. 'I don't remember stand-up arguments with Muff,' says Ian. 'But he'd come from Birmingham, was quite brusque, he just got on with it, did his thing... In actual fact Muff did a great job, and it was his experience of what works on a record that made a lot of those songs. "What a Way to End it All", for instance, was much more shambolic before he got his hands on it. And we play it his way to this day. But I remember there being bad feeling and I don't think it was ever quite resolved. Clive in particular was unhappy, but I think we all were, because we didn't have the experience.'

Derek Taylor wrote loyally of the sessions for *Melody Maker*. Being their label boss he was naturally biased, but his affection for Deaf School was sincere: 'The tapes are wonderful: fresh, original, different,' he reports of dropping by at Island Studios. 'I find the visit wholly satisfying. I love Deaf School. They will do well. There are only three of them at this session, Steve, Clive and Anne... There are seven others who are not there. Ten in all, hungry mouths, but not greedy and well worth feeding.'

Steve and Clive called in to the Warner office in New Oxford Street one day, with more tapes for Derek to hear: 'Derek had a lift from the ground floor straight into his office,' remembers Steve, 'and everyone else had another lift. So Clive and I were sitting in Derek's office, with the famous wicker chair that he took from Apple. He was plying us with a bit of Blue Nun or whatever they were drinking in those days. And we were playing him what we'd recorded with Muff. Next thing the lift opens and

George Harrison gets out. Derek obviously knew he was coming and goes, "Oh hullo George," and me and Clive are, "Uhhh, it's George Harrison!"

'Derek goes, "George, this is Deaf School that I was telling you about." And George goes, "Oh I've heard a lot about you guys." The track that's on is "Play it Again, Sam", and he goes, "What's this, the new Dylan album?" Derek says "No, this is Deaf School." "What, with that big Hammond on it?" And Clive said, "Yeah, we've got the Hammond." Anyway, George wasn't interested in hearing what we had to say. But he says to Clive, "*You're* not from Liverpool," and then he says to me, "*You* are, though."'

Recording was put on hold for a few weeks, before moving on 5 July to Orange Studios in New Compton Street and on 10 July to Air in Oxford Circus. Curiously, the new producer was to be Deaf School's head of publishing at Warners, Rob Dickins:

> I love Muff Winwood but I thought he missed who they were, and the record company weren't happy with what they had. I've seen this a lot with record companies. If everything doesn't fall into place straight away they move off, which is a danger.
>
> I'd produced a couple of little indie things, I knew nothing at all. But I knew these weren't right so I said to Derek Taylor, Give me Saturday in a cheap studio, I'll do one track and let's see if anything happens from that. We did 'Nearly Moonlit Night Motel' and it's basically the version that's on the record. It has a lot of flaws but it certainly captured who they were. So we did some more.
>
> I had a good chemistry with them in the studio and I had this engineer called Alan Winstanley

when I made my little records in a studio called TW [in Fulham]. So I used Alan Winstanley there and Steve Churchyard at Orange who went on to do Rod Stewart and everything else. So I had two engineers I was comfortable with, in cheap studios which kept the cost of making a record down.

If Rob Dickins was hardly a name producer, his musical roots were impressive. His father Percy Dickins had founded Britain's first music chart, at the *New Musical Express* in 1952. Rob's older brother, Barry, became a leading music agent of the 1960s and beyond, while Rob himself joined Warner Brothers in 1971, having been social secretary at Loughborough University. Within three years he was boss of the company's UK publishing arm. He has been a powerful figurehead of the British music industry ever since, playing a key part in the careers of Cher, Madonna, Rod Stewart and many more. And the Dickins dynastic reign continues: his nephew Jonathan, Barry's son, manages the vastly successful Adele. Barry's daughter Lucy is another music agent, with acts such as Hot Chip and Mumford & Sons. (Oh, and Rob is married to one of Pan's People.) But he admits that recording Deaf School was not easy:

They all wanted to be in different bands. When you worked closely with them you realised that Steve Lindsey wanted to be in 10cc, Clive wanted to be in Dr Feelgood and a bit later the Clash, Steve wanted to be in Roxy Music, the keyboard player wanted to be in the Bonzo Dog Band. So trying to harness their great energy was difficult, as they all pulled in different directions. But we finished the first record.

Clive and I spent a lot of time in the studio. For 'Where's the Weekend', we would spend hours trying to make it sound like 'Good Vibrations'. How did they do that? Or Abba: how do they get that sound? We loved the process, the experimentation. So we weren't just recording a live show, we were trying to create audio pictures. And Clive became obsessed with it. 'This is what I want to do.'

Clive's producing instinct was indeed awakened: 'When we started,' he says, 'there was no thought that we would make a record.

In those days I thought everyone had to *play*. Maybe I was listening to too much Mahavishnu Orchestra. We knew we were writing songs, but suddenly they were recordable: 'Oh, you *could* listen to this, with a bit of jiggery pokery.' Because I never saw myself as a pop star and I always wore glasses and I wasn't that great at playing, I always thought I'd be in the studio. I was always interested in listening to what the bass was playing on Beatles records, if there's a *clang* here or a *ding* there, what Beefheart was doing, how he got it. If you analyse it you can work out how he got it.

Was *2nd Honeymoon* the best Deaf School album? It is of course a matter of personal preference. What is objectively true, though, is that its songs were the most developed in their catalogue, fashioned from two years of stage performance. The record is not so much a series of songs as a theatrical revue. Busy and packed with pastiche, *2nd Honeymoon*'s extraneous details are so prevalent that they can distract from the album's core qualities. From the title track's *bar mitzvah* la-la-la's to the 'Wichita Lineman' steal in 'What a Way to End it All' (its banjo intro a vestige of Roy Holt's tenure), not forgetting some *Swan Lake*-quoting sax on 'Get Set Ready Go' (a snippet already borrowed on Roxy Music's first album) this was pure art school postmodernism. As ever with Deaf School, they were just a fraction too late to be innovators and three years too early to be mainstream.

With Langer and Allen taking the bulk of the writers' credits, melodic ingenuity and a love of story-telling are everywhere. Humour and feeling, not always found together, co-exist happily in these songs. Amid the comic posing and the musical costume changes are some glimpses of the authors' own emotional lives: Steve's Hockney-referencing 'Bigger Splash', as well as the title track, stem from his affair with Anne, while 'Knock Knock Knocking' was Clive's nod to an unhappy romance at Canterbury, its cruel comedy influenced by Ian Dury.

Sam Davis wrote the lyrics to another Deaf School evergreen, 'Hi Jo Hi'; its tune was a Clive Langer exercise in 'doing' Paul McCartney and took him, he says, all of five minutes. Its oddly discordant piano sections were influenced by Thunderclap Newman's 1969 hit 'Something in the Air' – and the net result was practically a blueprint for the future sound of Madness.

'Where's the Weekend' is a rare example of an all-band composition (or at least Clive/Enrico/Average/Bette) but its spirit is the payday hedonism of Scouse sailortown, channelled through Steve Allen. Night-time Liverpool weekends are practically a force of nature: civilian bystanders gawp in awe at a population's manic desire for entertainment. In this case an added refinement came from Derek Taylor: 'He was an elegant speaker,' says the lyricist. 'We were in the Orange studio, and I was coming up to the vocal, still messing about with the lyrics: "It's not what but who you know," and Derek said, "It's not really true that, you know." What? Maybe it should be, "It's not who but *what* you know." He saw the negative thing I was putting in, and he was right. He gave me a more positive song.'

Exquisitely sung by Bette Bright, 'Final Act' is the album's atmospheric closing number; its bittersweet portrayal of a fading actress would become a standard of the live repertoire. And its author was Steve Lindsey, emerging as a powerful third force in Deaf School's songwriting. 'I always wrote songs,' he says, 'and as the band gigged more, it was "OK, you've got a song, let's hear it." So I started chipping in, and the more you chip in, the more of a stake you have in it.'

'He didn't write a lot,' adds Enrico. 'It wasn't that he wrote songs and we rejected them. There was no ill-feeling like with George in the Beatles. He took a lot of care over writing a song. He liked to do it by himself and then come in with a complete thing. Whereas the rest of us would write *ensemble* a bit more.'

'Mine were fully formed songs,' agrees Mr Average. 'When I brought one, it was almost a *fait accompli*: This is how it goes, this is how we play it, these are the words. I think I've got more of an old-fashioned view of songwriting. And there's quite a few songs I brought to the table that just didn't have legs. Whereas with Clive's music, he would give you the black-and-white sketch and then say, "OK lads, colour it in." Songwriting-wise, what I contributed were little diversions.'

All they needed now was a cover to wrap it in. It was feared that a bulging collective of trained art theorists would never reach aesthetic agreement, but their friend Kevin Ward found his role surprisingly easy: 'The process was very un-democratic,' he says.

> Which for me, doing the artwork, was very lucky because designing by committee is a nightmare. All these things were new to us, but it just seemed fantastic to have a budget to do a proper record cover.
>
> It came about mainly through Steve's position in the band. He was the glamour boy up front, his image was Clark Gable as Rhett Butler. For me, '2nd Honeymoon' is their greatest song, and a brilliant title for an album. So the imagery came from that idea, married up to the *Gone With the Wind* poster, Rhett Butler holding Scarlet O'Hara and just about to come in for the big kiss. It was done with a back projection. Ideally, with a budget, we would have gone to somewhere like the West Indies, but that wasn't going to happen, so we bought a transparency from some agency, took the photo and on the back there's a load of people standing round, which was a way of getting a picture of the band in.

Enrico himself was pushing for 'something *kitsch*, kind of "Honey I'm home" America, because I was going through all that with the Hawaiian shirts. I was trying to be B-list Hollywood.' He's unsure why they went to an agency for his paramour: 'Maybe we still had two Bright Sisters when we planned it. I couldn't do it just with Sandra, or just with Bette. Or maybe it was because me and Bette were already an item but we didn't want to broadcast it. So we got this professional model to do it.'

Along with Rob Welch's Deaf School 'shield', which parodies the Warner Brothers logo, Kevin Ward's *2nd Honeymoon* design is probably the band's most enduring image. Where Roxy Music covers specialised in using unattainable beauties (on *For Your Pleasure*, even Bryan Ferry is reduced to the role of chauffeur), Deaf School's Enrico was the Scouse chancer who had blagged a photo opportunity. And where the front cover was utterly honest in its artifice, the back cover simply reinforced the process of de-mystification. Standing haphazardly around the cover stars, amid the studio paraphernalia, are the band members in their own chosen costumes: Bette as saucy housewife, Eric as lounge lizard, Average as film-lot lackey, and so on. The photography was by a Canterbury contact Colin Thomas.

'It was a good sleeve for a band coming out of Liverpool,' Enrico says. 'Not like a Manchester sleeve of a few years later. I think we were aware of that. Why should we look like some provincial band, just because we're not from London? We can be sophisticated, *kitsch* and witty. You can dare to be glamorous.' Its front façade and back 'reveal', he says, were adapted by Sheffield's ABC for their 1982 LP *The Lexicon of Love*, which is indeed strikingly similar.

2nd Honeymoon was released on 13 August 1976. Apart from its producers Rob Dickins and Muff Winwood, there were sleeve mentions for Ken Testi, Rob Welch and Kevin Ward, many departed band members (including 'Connie and all passing Bright Sisters') and 'Hope Street and the

Liverpool school'. But this album marked the end of Deaf School's Hope Street phase. Like an earlier Liverpool band, their immediate future lay downtown in Mathew Street, and thereafter the big wide world.

Unlike that earlier Liverpool band, though, Deaf School would find the times were not quite right. This was 1976, not 1963, and London at least had other things on its mind. 'It was actually pretty good, that album,' Bette Bright reflects. 'And then we won an award for the cover. Then what happened? Punk happened.'

FIVE

The Invisible River:
A Liverpool Interlude

Giving Up the Day Jobs – The Bowels of Mathew
Street – The Pool of Life and a Tub of Custard

A T THE BEGINNING OF 1976, nobody knew this would
be a watershed year in British pop music. Reigning
champions of the *Melody Maker* contest, Deaf School
looked as hot a prospect as any band in the land. Holding
court in the Phil, Cracke or Belvedere, they were no longer
art students in a band, but professional musicians, with
a contract from the world's most famous entertainment
company.

There was the novel experience of having some money.
Clive Langer: 'Steve and I got a 20 grand advance when
we first signed our publishing to Warners, and we just
spent it on a PA, ploughed it into the band. Basically we
lost it, which was fine, we never thought about it. We

were on £25 a week and the two married members, Sam and John, were on £75 a week. Twenty-five a week was enough to live in Princes Avenue. One week I'd be in the Neal Street restaurant in London with Derek and the next night would be chips and curry sauce around the Rialto.'

Enrico strolled the boulevards of Liverpool 8 in pyjamas and a tweed overcoat. Anne Martin's friend from Canterbury, Dave Sargeant, loved to explore the city with her: 'You know what Liverpudlians are like. They would all shout out "Bette Bright!" You were the bee's knees to be walking around with her.'

For Max Ripple it was finally time to give up the day job: 'Sam/Eric and I both had kids and we both had salaries when we got the Warner Brothers deal. Sam was a teacher in several schools in the area. So we were the only two who were fully salaried, and we got the same or more than we were getting as teachers. Looking back, it was incredibly generous of the band. So I had in my passport, "Entertainer". Which was very nice.

'It was a funny thing, being professional and doing something like this. The same with shamanism: to keep things alive, you need to know a bit but you shouldn't know too much. And I don't think we knew much!'

An issue of Liverpool's *The Last Trumpet* fanzine, put together in early 1976, was devoted to these big-shot Warner signings Deaf School as they prepared their first album. 'I guess I'm just an old romantic at heart,' wrote Enrico. 'Bring back wooing in the moonlight, picnics and strolls under the stars on the beach, and rock on with *2nd Honeymoon*.' On the verge of punk, a less 1976 manifesto it's hard to imagine. There was also an ad for their forthcoming show with Scaffold, at the Philharmonic

Hall on 3 July. It was to be promoted by the man behind *The Last Trumpet* itself, one Roger Eagle (of whom, more in a moment). And on page 11 was a plug for something called the Liverpool School of Language, Music, Dream & Pun. This was in fact an old warehouse at 18 Mathew Street, a few doors down from the Cavern. It had been leased since 1974 by a local poet named Peter Halligan (sometimes O'Halligan), who ran it as a kind of HQ for young Liverpool dreamers.

The downstairs part of O'Halligan's, as the place was normally called, was given over to a market named Aunt Twacky's (a play on the Scouse slang 'antwacky', for antique). Vintage clothes were the speciality, including those vibrant Hawaiian shirts favoured by Enrico Cadillac. And upstairs was a café, the Parlour, which could double as a theatre or rehearsal space. It was like a scruffy little piece of Liverpool 8, transported down the hill into town. And then Peter's cousin, Sean Halligan, mentioned a book by Carl Gustav Jung, the Swiss psychiatrist. At which point things *really* turned strange.

***

In 1927 Jung had a vivid dream of being in 'a dirty, sooty city' that he came to understand was Liverpool: amid its squalor he had a sudden vision of 'unearthly beauty' at the city's core. Awakening, he declared Liverpool 'the Pool of Life'. It occurred to Peter Halligan that the space outside his building, where Mathew Street converges with several others in this little warren of backstreets, had the pentagram-like quality that Jung described. And, as archaeologists knew, beneath a nearby manhole ran the remains of a lost tidal inlet: the Pool. Peter and Sean seized upon the notion, baptised their warehouse the Liverpool School of Language, Music, Dream & Pun and set up a bust of Carl Jung on the wall outside.

The Pool is not imaginary. It gave the city its name. Boats once sailed right up this lost branch of the Mersey, and a bridge would cross it at the bottom of Lord Street. It was built over and its mouth converted into the first of the Liverpool docks, the first of its kind in the world. You can still trace the valley of this invisible river, from the waterfront, up Paradise Street and Whitechapel, as far as the Mersey Tunnel. You could say it was the Rubicon crossed by Brian Epstein, on the day he walked from his NEMS shop on the far side of Whitechapel to see the Beatles in a damp cellar on the Pool's western bank. Basements in Mathew Street are prone to flooding. At O'Halligan's they said it was the Pool reclaiming its space.

The Halligans had in fact imported uptown art-think into the heart of Scouse downtown. Conversations in the tea-room ran from occult coincidences (the numbers 5 and 23 were especially popular) and conspiracy theories, to the sort of Celtic dreaming and stoned romanticism that are innate in Scousers and highly attractive to a certain type of outsider, who finds in it a respite from Anglo-Saxon realism. Deaf School were probably fated to make this building their new home. Before long, they colonised the school's upper floor for rehearsals and performance. And, as we've seen, it was on this spot that Brian Epstein's ghost-writer Derek Taylor fell in love with the band.

Bernie Connor, then a city centre schoolboy, remembers, 'Me and my mates used to go and see them on Thursday nights at Aunt Twacky's. I was only about 14, everyone was older than me, but I never felt intimidated. It was so welcoming. And they were great. There were loads of them.'

The school's public launch came with the inaugural Jung Festival, held in Mathew Street on 6 June 1976. Deaf School performed from a makeshift stage whose parts were borrowed from nearby building sites: 'That was a special moment,' Clive remembers. 'First song we did, Tim got off his drum kit and sang "The Jung Ones".' Roy and Sandra had left the band, but Paul Pilnick was on board and a temporary Bright Sister, Lynn McKay, was there to partner Bette. Also playing were local busker act the Picasso Sisters and Deaf School's art college allies Albert Dock. The latter band's Henry Priestman, who would soon be in the Yachts and later the Christians, recalls of that day: 'All I know is, Mr Langer was the first person who said to me, "Why don't you write your *own* songs" ... Cheers Clive, I owe you one – a big one!'

Deaf School fan Laurence Sidorczuk hitched over from Manchester art school: 'It was a fantastic day, a beautiful warm, sunny afternoon and evening, crowds of people. Not too long after I was invited by Sean Halligan to join with him and Peter at the Liverpool School of Language, Music, Dream & Pun. And that became my base. Peter Halligan had done an exhibition about Carl Jung and the Liverpool Dream. On the day, he invited Carl Jung's grandson over to unveil the bust of Jung in the niche. He also invited the Swiss Consul. Peter and a lot of other people were dressed in Swiss Navy uniforms. There being no such thing as a Swiss Navy.'

***

Meanwhile, up in Hope Street, the Liverpool School's surrealist radicalism had a more political counterpart in the Everyman Theatre. The 1970s were a great time for this hotbed of innovation, the early home of so many famous names including Willy Russell, Jonathan Pryce, Julie Walters, Alan Bleasdale, Jim Broadbent, Bernard Hill and Pete Postlethwaite. 'The theatre group at the time was great,' Clive Langer told the *Daily Post* in 2011. 'People like Julie Walters and Bill Nighy, and I remember going to see their plays. It was a bit of a scene, really. We were the musicians and they were the actors and we would end up at the same parties.'

Later that year, in November, O'Halligan's hosted the Science Fiction Theatre of Liverpool. Formed by the director and playwright Ken Campbell, with the actor Chris Langham, the project employed a host of Everyman regulars (including Bill Drummond, ex-of Liverpool art school, then working as a set-builder). With the additional help of budding musicians such as Jayne Casey, Ian Broudie and Budgie, Campbell conceived a nine-hour series of plays called *Illuminatus*. Based on a trilogy of cult novels by the American writers Robert Shea and Robert Anton Wilson, it was more anarchic than the Everyman's brand of tough comedy and social realism.

Deaf School were in effect just one more aspect of the energies of Hope Street, flowing down to the Pool to lap against the Mathew Street bank. Even so, the band resisted Beatles associations. Says Enrico:

> The thing about Deaf School was there was only me and Average who were local. We didn't consciously *not* do the Beatles, we liked them, but there's no actual Beatles thread running though, unless it's

pastiche. The Beatle suit was our nod, our ironic take on it. But it had to be Average in a Beatles suit because of his connection with Paul and Mike. We encouraged him: 'Why don't you get a left-handed Hofner bass?'

Average was still in touch with Paul McCartney's close-knit Wirral clan: 'Through the family I got to meet Paul on loads of occasions. The nice thing is that as Deaf School developed and I was part of the Robbins/McCartney set-up, Paul did take an interest, it'd be "How's the band going?" when you met him on New Year's Eve at the family gathering. He was always interested in what was going on.'

The local promoter Roger Eagle had definitely set his face against Fab Four nostalgia. Now he shaped a musical regeneration of Mathew Street, just a few yards from the site of its holiest shrine. Eagle was a former DJ, from Oxford via Manchester, whose time at the latter city's Twisted Wheel Club was central to the rise of Northern Soul, helped along by his vast knowledge of music and crusading zeal for sharing it around. He cut a tall, *film noir* figure, hunched over his glowing spliff, squinting in its smoke, speaking quietly with deadpan intensity. And his instinct was that Deaf School were harbingers of something important.

When the Stadium began winding down, Eagle diversified into Thursday night shows at the Metro, a basement club in Sweeting Street, by Liverpool Town Hall. As guaranteed crowd-pullers, Deaf School were his failsafe, with admission fixed at 75 pence (twice the price of their Back of the Moon shows a year earlier). The club's strong similarity to the Beatles-era Cavern is captured in a stage photo for the *2nd Honeymoon* inner sleeve, taken by the band's friend Monty Rakusen. According to his long-serving ally Doreen Allen, Roger liked to think of Deaf School as his house band.

Sandy Bright performed here with the band in the period between the sacking of her boyfriend Roy Holt and her own departure. One night, from the stage, she spotted Roy in conversation with an ex-girlfriend, stormed off through the crowd and gave him a slap. Another night, Mr Average had just missed a run of rehearsals at O'Halligan's because of the flu. To his horror the band went into a new song he didn't know, "Princess Princess", so he simply walked off and joined the audience. 'And it was the only time in my life I've ever seen Deaf School. I was very impressed.'

Ken Testi had come to know Roger Eagle well through the Stadium and Metro periods, and they decided it was time for an emerging new audience to have its own home. In that eventful punk summer of 1976 the pair found premises in Mathew Street, right opposite the old Cavern (now filled with rubble and awaiting final demolition). In fact their chosen venue was its successor club, the New Cavern, owned by a well-known player in the city's nightlife, Roy Adams. The cellar room had recently been relaunched as the Revolution, with giant fibreglass heads of Fidel Castro and Che Guevara joining an older semi-relief of the Beatles in mop-top guise. Upstairs was a more conventional nightclub called Gatsby's, with ground-level access from Victoria Street. Roger and Ken would have preferred Gatsby's, for its ease of 'get-in'. But that was not to be.

Instead they renamed the basement club Eric's, a wry Testi joke on chic joints like Annabel's and its imitators. (There was also a popular tailor called Eric's, up by Lime Street.) Before the downstairs venue was ready, Deaf

School played a pre-opening night in Gatsby's. On the next night, 1 October, the Stranglers played the same stage for Eric's official unveiling, followed a week later by all-girl US act the Runaways (hurriedly booked by Ken after he saw their picture in the *NME*). On 15 October, when upstairs was still used for the headlining acts, the Sex Pistols played their only Liverpool show.

Now downstairs and joined by a third partner, Pete Fulwell, Eric's at last went nightly. Deaf School's PA, enormous and painted blue, was stored on the premises when they were not touring and offered to local musicians for daytime practice. ('We referred to this as "growing our own",' says Ken.) That same October, Geoff Davies opened a new branch of Probe Records, on a prominent corner site a few yards away from Mathew Street, by the White Star pub. The Beatles' old haunts were falling, one by one, to the new wave. By an ironic quirk, there was a Beatles memorial high on the wall above Eric's, sculpted by Arthur Dooley for the building's New Cavern period. It suddenly looked forlorn.

***

In time the Beatles trade would thoroughly revive and reclaim its own, but it was Deaf School, Probe and the Halligans' Liverpool School which started Mathew Street's renaissance. Eric's itself is now remembered as a punk venue, but that's only because punk and new wave music dominated those years. The founders' vision (and 'vision' is not, in this case, a silly word for it) was of a place that made exploration possible and discoveries would follow. Eagle and his DJs created a soundtrack of dub reggae, vintage soul, crackpot rockabilly and obscure psychedelia. As with the mods of the Twisted Wheel, he liked to share his musical inspirations. Ken Testi, meanwhile, was teasingly reminded to keep his old Queen connection quiet.

In Liverpool the veneration of outsider artists like Captain Beefheart and Arthur Lee of Love was something shared between the *ateliers* of Canning Street and the suburban estates. The next generation of acts, from Echo & the Bunnymen to Frankie Goes To Hollywood, grew up with grand aesthetic notions, even without art school theory. Given enough to smoke, this took on a quasi-spiritual aspect that was sometimes dubbed 'cosmic scally'.

In 1976 Liverpudlian whimsy met Jungian mysticism and got along famously. The combination found a receptive audience in non-Scousers like Bill Drummond and Julian Cope. (Drummond would later pick up this ball and run a long way with it, encouraging a mythology around the Bunnymen and Teardrops that featured global ley lines meeting in Mathew Street.) Of Deaf School's members, Max Ripple was the most intrigued: 'That to me was a kind of magic period. It coincided with the Jung Festival. So these are the big dimensions, if you're mapping or looking for the alignment of different things. It was a very ambitious idea, with the Beat poets in America and Liverpool and Jung, mapping the John Lennon ley line.'

O'Halligan's became the Armadillo Tea Rooms and continued as a drop-in centre for the sort of people whose world was now defined by Probe, 100 yards to the left, and Eric's, 100 yards to the right. There were two more Jung Festivals. The third, in 1978, is mainly remembered for one of the Liverpool School's organisers, Charles Gilmour-Alexander, diving into a giant skip of custard.

SIX

Hypertension

Punk and Unpunk – The Time Out of
Joint – Don't Stop the World

D EAF SCHOOL'S FIRST ALBUM had not been easy to make.
It had involved the rebellion of an entirely inexperienced band against their label-appointed producer, a
man with rather more chart success to his name than they
had. Even after a change of producer, *2nd Honeymoon*
was not the sound that most band members still longed
to hear. But that was by the by. What mattered now was
the opinion of the outside world.

As usual, the first public response was from the weekly
music press, which in 1976 was at the historic height of
its prestige. Just before the album's release, *Melody Maker*
again put Deaf School on its cover, trailing an arguably
premature piece on Liverpool's resurgence as a musical

powerhouse. (While Toxteth soulsters the Real Thing were breaking big, the Eric's generation was as yet unborn; Deaf School's art school colleagues Nasty Pop, namechecked on the *2nd Honeymoon* cover, had signed with Island but to no great success.) The paper was quick to remind its readers that Deaf School were the winners of the previous year's Rock and Folk contest. But that was then and this was 1976; 'Ramones Are Rubbish' went a reader's letter on the back page, typical of the controversies now raging in rock. (Curiously, its author was a future production client of Clive Langer, one 'Steve Morrissey' of Stretford, Manchester. Touchingly, he was declared an 'LP Winner'.)

The *Maker*'s actual review appeared a few weeks later and was moderately encouraging: 'A successful and entertaining debut,' it concluded. Barbara Charone, writing in *Sounds* the same week, took the praise up a few notches: 'Easily one of the most impressive first albums I've heard in a long time.' Few magazines used star ratings in those days, but *Sounds* did. She gave it five, the maximum.

Rather ominously, the most influential and by now biggest-selling paper of all, the *NME*, didn't get around to Deaf School for another month. The review was assigned to an older freelancer, Bob Edmands, an entertaining writer but quite outside the paper's central committee of taste-makers. With no axe to grind or punk credentials to claim, he was supportive without overt enthusiasm: 'With the right handling Deaf School could prove to be very deft, indeed.'

But reviews were not everything. 'Features', the interview-based articles that took up the front half of each paper, were far more indicative of a band's status, and front covers were most important of all. On 13 November

1976, some time after the album's promotional push, the *NME* found a small amount of feature space for Deaf School, in an issue that captures the tensions of its time. There was, for example, an evident disconnect between editorial and advertising. A fervent profile of the Damned, by the punky young reporter Tony Parsons, lurks near a record company push for Jon Lord's 'baroque dance suite' *Sarabande.* Then there were the normal small ads at the back of the paper, offering 'split knee denim jeans' and cheesecloth shirts, as if the punk aesthetic of Malcolm McLaren's and Vivienne Westwood's Sex shop had never existed.

The short interview with Deaf School itself sits opposite a full-page advert for Queen, a flamboyant band defiantly at odds with the *NME*'s newly acquired punk purism. (Few would have noticed that the two acts had an obscure connection, through Ken Testi and Brian May.) Deaf School's treatment by their interviewer Angus MacKinnon reflects an *NME* view that this band were already out of date. Even if they weren't exactly hippies, they were not true punks. Enrico is held to represent old-fashioned escapism, a charge he readily accepts: 'Personally I consider my stuff about beaches and honeymoons to be a lot less corny than most rock lyrics anyway,' he asserts, citing his dad's show business values as an enduring influence. 'I'm not really in love with the modern world. I like the old things and old movies… The entertainment and cabaret side of things is what appeals to me. I think of myself as an entertainer in the traditional British sense.'

MacKinnon, a measured and cerebral writer, without punk pretensions, does pay tribute to Clive Langer's musical stewardship. 'If his playing was ever less than energetic,' he writes, 'then the whole elaborate edifice would simply crumple, all the visuals notwithstanding.' When pushed, Clive is quoted as agreeing that the first album lacks emotion, pleading that the band were too inexperienced at the time of recording. Perhaps we can detect here two rival forces in the band's make-up: Enrico's taste for romantic nostalgia against Clive's yearning for greater rock urgency.

But far worse for band morale had been a *Melody Maker* piece by Richard Williams, in the issue of 28 August. To this day it's the single piece of media coverage that bothers Deaf School the most. Williams had in 1971 been the first mainstream writer to predict success for the unsigned Roxy Music. Then in 1973 he crossed the floor to become an A&R man at Island, where he expressed interest in signing Deaf School, before returning to full-time journalism. Like his colleague Chris Welch, who had written most of *Melody Maker*'s genially uncritical coverage of Deaf School, Williams was of the pre-punk generation. But like the DJ John Peel, he was sincerely committed to acceptance of the new, even at the expense of the old. This was a tiny culture war, and Deaf School were about to become collateral damage.

In Williams' regular column, that week called 'Let's Have A Generation Gap Again', he welcomes the dumb energy of punk as a purgative and counterweight to ageing 'progressive' tastes. Unfortunately, he selects two young art rock bands, Deaf School and New Zealand's Split Enz, to represent an alleged dead end. (Split Enz had just made their second LP, *Mental Notes*, produced by Roxy's Phil Manzanera. Ironically, with the addition of Neil Finn, the group became the nucleus of the extremely successful

Crowded House.) He talks of meeting Deaf School at Derek Taylor's launch party, twelve months after watching them at the Back of the Moon: 'It was easy to see that the year had taken its toll: a year of, among other things, firing musicians because they weren't up to professional standards, a year of learning the realities of "Making it".'

The article, says Clive Langer, 'was like the beginning of the end for us. It was weird, because Richard had wanted us to sign to Island, but he really put a downer on Deaf School with this article about how great the Pistols were and how shit we were.' Though well-argued, the column was another indication of how dangerously fast the tides of London taste could change.

Commentary on rock culture, in 1976, was dominated by the weekly music papers. There were as yet no glossy monthlies, and mainstream media paid little attention, except for the occasional blaze of shock and horror. The *NME* in particular had a remarkable mix of hip authority and rebellious wit, though the younger and even brasher paper, *Sounds*, was snapping at its heels. *Melody Maker*, the oldest and most venerable weekly, was undergoing internal debate but overall remained steadfast to establishment acts like Jethro Tull and Eric Clapton. Nevertheless, its support for Deaf School had been valuable, and to see that slip away was worrying.

*** *

That summer, I was chosen by *NME* as one of its new intake of journalists, dubbed 'hip young gunslingers'. Hired on the strength of a sample piece about Deaf School's heroes Kilburn & the High Roads, I was promised some lowly paid freelance work (the staff jobs were given to a couple who soon became the prime pundits of punk, Tony Parsons and Julie Burchill). But I keenly set about posting my amateur efforts, including several reviews from Eric's club. There was no response. Whatever I sent to the *NME* disappeared into some black hole. Among my ignored experiments in one-fingered typing was this appreciation of Deaf School:

> Funny things happen in Liverpool pubs. You order your brown-bitter and notice you're standing next to a vicar in make-up. With a large badge saying Deaf School, he might be collecting for charity, a trendy cleric or a Rag Week prankster. But my best friend put me right. 'Art school' he whispered. One understood.
>
> Sure enough there was the Rev Max Ripple a few nights later, playing keyboards and arch-divvy for this group of Hope Street sophistos. Maybe a dozen strong they served up some Rock *aux* Bonzos with many a passing nod to Scaffold and Liverpool Scene. From the club'n'college circuit, of course, Deaf School went on to win a v. prestigious Competition, met that wittiest of Beatlepeople Derek Taylor and joined the Brothers Warner. The rest is Publicity.
>
> Justified? Well, I doubt even the *Please Please Me* LP would have merited the vast hoo-hah laid on for *2nd Honeymoon*. Chances are you've all seen Enrico Cadillac Jnr, smooching in delectable Technicolor over two-thirds of your record shop window lately. Obviously someone's got faith in abundance that Deaf School have got that which it takes.
>
> Gone are some of the human props that decorated their set a while back. Emphasis is now on front-person

Enrico Cadillac, a boyish warbler with a Clark Gable fixation, a (Bryan) Ferry Across The Mersey. Eric is all an Eric should be. In Flemings or Tux, he does have class. Bette Bright is one to watch. On stage the Bright Sisters' spirited attack on 'Midnight Hour' is a revelation. Her 'Hi Jo Hi' provides the album with its absolute high, a natural single and just what Deaf School do best. 'Final Act' has Bette as a cracked actress, sung with Dietrich-like melancholy. Quite a voice.

I do like Enrico. He comes on like he's just walked off the cover of *Another Time Another Place*, singing of posh hotels, special romances and make it one for the road, would you, bar-chappie? He's so utterly inauthentic it's likeable. Like a village drama club stab at Noel Coward's *Blithe Spirit*. Through every 'such a bore' and 'simply divine' (and there are lots) those muddy Scouse vowels and two-ton consonants come out. Thankfully, you know he knows we know. No attempt is made to impress, only amuse. Pretension is punctured throughout – check out the back cover of that album sleeve. Deaf School walk the line.

Well, I made perhaps one valid point. There is a keen wariness of 'hype' among committed music fans. The core rock audience, the early adopters, like to feel they've discovered a secret. Deaf School's Liverpool fans thought they'd done exactly that: they'd found a raw, home-grown talent. But nationally, people believed the band were the artificial creations of Warner Brothers. They looked at the generous marketing campaign and they smelled Bugs Bunny's money.

I hoped to dispel that impression. In particular, we Liverpool followers had always understood the charm of Enrico Cadillac. Where London critics saw a poseur pretending to sophistication, and disapproved, we saw a Scouse dandy putting on a show. And we approved completely. Local writer John McCready wrote in *The Word* many years later: 'Steve Allen became Enrico Cadillac Jnr, a Clark Gable in eyeliner channelling Bryan Ferry while drinking brown-mixed.'

Deaf School's Scouse fans found the make-believe emancipating. It was our little window on to a world delineated by Noel Coward and Hollywood, by glamour and intelligence; and Enrico was the key because we knew he was one of us. The rest of the band we couldn't guess at, but Enrico we recognised as a charming impostor. As soon as he spoke, with *that* accent, it was not a moment of exposure but of connection.

Despairing of the *NME*'s indifference, I then tried *Sounds*, and favoured them with this review from my college, the London School of Economics:

'It's fab in here tonight, isn't it?' ventured Frank Average, the eternal Beatle fan. And I couldn't see anyone in the jam-packed LSE theatre who wasn't inclined to agree with him. It was fab, all right, and maybe the happiest gig I'd seen in a long time. Just a few months in smelling distance of the Big Time have transformed Deaf School from a cute gang of art college jokers into a tight, sophisticated musical force.

Drawing mostly from the debut album *2nd Honeymoon* they presented a set that featured the non-stop kitsch'n'camp that's expected of them, but which was ultimately memorable for the sheer rock'n'roll power they're rapidly learning to generate.

'Hi Jo Hi' provided perhaps the best example of what Deaf School are about, lively and infectious with the visual action bouncing between Bette, Enrico and Eric like a pin-ball. Next came 'It Should've been Mo (With that Real Fine Chick)' which was OK but suffered, I thought, from being too good-humoured: I missed the sour envious touch that gives an edge to the Commander Cody version. They go into 'Nearly Moonlit Night Motel' in which the vocal trio indulge their fondness for hammy theatrics. 'O-oh! A-ah!' they moan: the effect is deliberately bad B-movie.

But now it's the turn of the Rev. Max Ripple to take a bow. Donning his accordion and assuming his drippiest clerical tones, he introduces Bette Bright who re-emerges with a new costume and new persona for 'Final Act'. The girl's got a truly remarkable voice that, for my money, makes her the School's Star Pupil. It's the perfect complement to the power trio of Langer, Lindsey and Whittaker who form the band's musical backbone. Add the Reverend's keyboards and Ian Ritchie's sax to give –

Here alas the surviving manuscript ends, a loss to literature we can bear with fortitude. *Sounds* ignored it, anyway, probably because the same gig was reviewed by their own reviewer, Barbara Charone. (For the record, she took the same enthusiastic view of Deaf School that I had.) By the time I was finally writing for the *NME*, it was too late to help Deaf School. They had few other media champions.

Chronologically the band's career overlapped closely with that of the Sex Pistols, and both had art school origins. In Jon Savage's book *England's Dreaming*, the London group's manager Malcolm McLaren says, 'I learned all my politics and understanding of the world through the history of art.' In 2006 he told the *Radio Times*: 'People remember punk from a musical perspective, but to me it was an artistic movement.' In reality, punk would draw support from all sorts of people, from real anarchists to football hooligans. But McLaren was the arch-theorist of its early emergence in Britain.

Despite the fact that many of the first punks were art students (including the Pistols' chief writer Glen Matlock), the movement liked to play down that association, because it lacked the desired aura of street credibility. Typical of the time was a passing remark from the *NME* that Deaf School 'is an unwieldy nine-piece and they stand around in untidy clumps, dressed haphazardly in the sort of gear students adopt for rag days'. McLaren's brand of punk sprang from a West London scene of perhaps no more than 30 artistic socialites (dubbed 'Them' in a 1976 essay by Peter York) whose reference points had been Roxy Music and Biba. But Deaf School were outsiders, whose art college provenance was only too well known. Punk's impulse was a stripping-down: it was almost puritanical. But Deaf School were multi-faceted: they were romantics, not roundheads.

Concealing one's education and middle-class background was as much a punk habit as shaving a few years off your age and burning the old photos of your band with long hair and loon-pants. Deaf School had been around in the public eye just a little too long to attempt such Stalinist rewriting of their history. They couldn't cover their traces even if they'd wished to. They were also too steeped in a tradition of art school music that loved pastiche and slapstick more than it revelled in aggression. The irony is that living in Liverpool 8, Deaf School saw rather more working-class reality than the media-savvy squat-dwellers of Kensington and Chelsea.

Max Ripple points out, with clerical mildness, that it's all a bit rich, considering the Sex Pistols used to come and watch Deaf School. This is quite true. At the Nashville pub in West Kensington, for example, before the Pistols were christened, their guitarist Steve Jones was making coarse heckles about Bette, to chivalrous Enrico's annoyance. Nor, as Max says, were Deaf School themselves ignorant of the Pistols' own work. 'And the Damned,' he adds. 'Yes of course Clive went to see all of them, and both Steves. It felt like we were under attack, that's my recollection. For being glam-rock, "the art school band." I think it's a valid point. There's a side of Roxy Music that is very bourgeois.'

But in rock's small sub-culture, hip taste alternates between artifice and authenticity. In 1976, four years on from Roxy Music's debut, the ball had very much bounced back to the 'authentic' side of the court. The distinction is largely bogus: there was plenty of contrivance in supposedly un-styled acts such as Bruce Springsteen and Dire Straits, just as there was real emotional heft in the records of David Bowie and Roxy Music. But in popular discourse the question goes, 'Is this band for real, or are they just posing?'

The London/Liverpool distinction was vexing. Deaf

School were scarcely yokels, and never dressed as such, and their personal links with the capital were still strong. Clive Langer:

> We'd walk into gigs and people would go, Fuck, look at what they're wearing! We were something completely new and different. And London kind of embraced it. We'd go to Acme Attractions [a Kings Road shop] and they'd know who we were. I'd go there and buy shoes. I knew what was going on in London cos I was still connected. So we were this new thing, but then the punk tsunami was so strong, we couldn't fight it. We were considered by some of our audience as punk. We definitely had a punky side, wearing ties and jackets, it's just we had that cabaret side, Steve's love of the 1940s and 50s, his pale blue suit was a Sinatra copy. Then you got people like Dave Vanian [singer of the Damned] and it all made sense, the dark eye make-up, we were all connected, but we didn't get the press on our side in London, at all.

As they had in Liverpool, Deaf School won admirers in Britain's grittier outposts, where their escapist glamour would find its echoes in the 1980s 'new romantic' movement – too late, of course, for the band to capitalise upon. 'It was like that in South Wales, by the way,' says Enrico.

> We were massive there, people like Chris Sullivan, Steve Strange [future luminaries of the new romantics]. Places like Merthyr Tydfil, proud and rough boxing communities, mining communities. These were tough places and they were loving the glamour of Roxy Music. The make-up. I remember

Deaf School going to play in Merthyr a big crowd, more dressed up than we were. They'd come from all different parts of Wales to the gig because they knew it was the only place where they could all be outrageous, wear make-up and not get beaten up.

When punk rock broke big in media and commercial terms, throughout 1977, it caused consternation among the rock hierarchy. With the conceivable exception of David Bowie, whose own appeal was still unique, older British acts from Paul McCartney and Pete Townshend to Rick Wakeman and the Moody Blues wondered if their time was over. In the event they were able to ride out the storm without too much difficulty. The real victims of this sudden sea-change were younger bands whose image did not fit the new dispensation, and Deaf School may be the best example.

Watching supportively from afar, the band's former flugelhorn player Hazel Bartram could sense the time was out of joint for Deaf School. On graduating from the art college, she had spent some time doing voluntary work with kids in Liverpool 8, where she'd encountered deprivation that shocked her. 'The culture was so obviously changing,' she says. 'Young people's lives were becoming so much harder, and they wanted music to reflect that.'

***

In the face of media scepticism, it would have helped if Deaf School had the solid support of their record company. Alas, not even Warner Brothers were entirely on board. Bette remembers seeing dissent as early as their celebratory show in Liverpool the previous December.

'People like Dave Dee [a Warner exec and former pop star, leader of Dozy, Beaky, Mick & Titch], he never liked us. A lot of those people never liked us. We were Derek's baby. He loved us. We did that gig at the Everyman when we signed, and everyone came up from Warners to see it. But some of them didn't get it.'

As Steve 'Average' Lindsey explains:

> It was a worldwide deal but the contract was actually with Warners in LA, at Burbank. I know now the way these things work with record companies, there may have been a little bit of resentment in the London office that they were being obliged to spend x amount of money on this band that they didn't actually sign. I think we would have benefited from some strong A&R from the record company, or from stronger management with a creative streak, the sounding board that bands and artists really thrive upon. Derek Taylor was very supportive, but he admired the band rather than anything else.

Mysteriously, the question of Deaf School's name was suddenly posed as a problem. Nobody had thought to mention it before. As Bette says: 'Because we were in "the Deaf School" it wasn't like a weird name, it didn't mean anything.' On the other hand, when Warners invited Deaf School to see the company's new signing Al Jarreau, the band were surprised to find the front two rows of Ronnie Scott's reserved for them: 'We were sitting right by the bloody speakers. And it's because they thought we were all deaf!'

Rob Dickins, by now Deaf School's in-house producer at Warners, recalls the promotion department's misgivings:

As the first record came out a few things happened. The beginnings of punk were quite exciting. And the other thing was they were called Deaf School. Radio 1– and this was before they'd even banned Frankie Goes To Hollywood – Radio 1 had made Ray Davies change Coca-Cola to cherry cola [in the Kinks' song *Lola*]. They were very powerful and they had these edicts, 'We're not gonna play any records by a band called Deaf School.'

So we had to have a crisis meeting at Warner Brothers. 'What are we gonna do?' We had a record that people were going to love. We hadn't been steamrollered by punk yet. But there were no other radio stations, really, no regional ways of breaking records, no internet. Quite a good fan-base, they were selling out 1000 to 1500-seaters on tour. So we had to decide whether we called it Deaf School. The promotion department were absolute that we had to change the name.

A few names were bandied around and I felt very hollow through it. I hated every name put forward. Derek Taylor was refereeing all this. I had always loved the fact it was music and it was called Deaf School: we told Radio 1 there was a reason for it, this is where they rehearsed, and so on. But I secretly liked having a band called Deaf School, and I couldn't be swayed from it. Not that I had a lot of say, but I was young, I was principled and felt that these idiots at Radio 1 can't tell you what you call yourself. And Derek came down on that side: 'I agree. We signed a band called Deaf School, they made a record and we should stick by them.'

> So that was a major issue. And we never got any
> Radio 1 play.

Average remembers the band digging their heels in: 'It wasn't as clear-cut as changing the name. It was bowing down to The Man. That was the first time we wondered if we'd done the right thing, signing to this lot rather than to Virgin. But the same thing might have happened there. But we were too attached to the name. And we'd done all those gigs, it would have felt like a betrayal of the fans we already had.'

* * *

Deaf School's second album is overshadowed by their first because it lacks the vivid, cinematic story-lines of *2nd Honeymoon*'s songs – songs that remain the basis of a great, as-yet unwritten musical. *Don't Stop the World* itself has a couple of songs that would be indispensable to such a show. The band themselves are mostly protective of its memory. But it was certainly a troubled creation, and left an ambivalent legacy.

An early omen of misfortune was Max Ripple's enforced absence from part of its recording. 'He contracted some exotic disease,' says Average. 'We were still based in Liverpool and got into the minibus to a London gig: in the van you could see he was going green, pale blue, purple, he was in such a bad way. We arrived at the hotel and the doctor had to be called. Before the gig that evening, Clive said, "Get a couple of beers inside you, you'll be fine." But he was so ill that we did the gig that evening without him. Which was weird, because even though there's loads of people in

Deaf School it's still quite strange when the keyboard's missing.

'He ended up being in quarantine in a special hospital, for about a month. He was in a real bad way, had to be separated from the world. And during this period we were recording the second album and Mike Barson's brother Ben came in to do keyboards, so if you look at the credits you'll see him as guest musician.' ['Due to Max's rest in Neasden Isolation Hospital.'] Another substitution was Danny Adler, borrowed from Roogalator, who deputised for the recently departed Paul Pilnick. Recording took place in Sarm East studio, at the bottom of Brick Lane in Whitechapel, in those days an area still morbidly defined by the Krays. Final sessions were done at Scorpio, under the Capital Radio HQ in Euston Road.

'The record company wanted us to do a second album really quickly,' says Average. 'I think *Don't Stop the World* suffers because it's rushed, and even though we'd written lots of material, that material seemed to be redundant because the punk thing had begun to play a really big role. It doesn't work as well as it should have done, because we felt obliged to leave a lot of *2nd Honeymoon* behind us, a lot of that character and theatre. We thought if we'd persevered with a development of *2nd Honeymoon*, we'd have been laughed out of the country. So it was a no-win situation. The record company wanted a quick record and a cheaper record, because *2nd Honeymoon* cost them a lot of money and it hadn't sold the quantities that Warner Brothers were expecting.'

As Rob Dickins remembers, Warners were moderately encouraged by the first album and Derek Taylor was still sufficiently in charge to protect the band's interests.

But a lot had happened in the twelve months since *2nd Honeymoon* was recorded, whether in the world outside or within Deaf School itself. 'All the differences were really now showing,' he says.

The band that put together the first album was much more a unit than on the second album. So it was very much me and Clive and Steve. By that time punk was getting off the ground and Clive really wanted to be in a punk band. Steve was still the crooner in a Roxy Music vein. Though he and Clive were very close; we'd go to the Roxy [the punk club in Covent Garden] to see bands. Clive became more than ever the leader and took them more into a punk direction with tracks like 'Capaldi's Café'. Trying to emulate Eddie & the Hot Rods, that bridge of pub-rock into punk.

At the same time, Steve always had a thing for those grand opus pop songs like 'Eloise' [a mock-operatic hit for Barry Ryan in 1968]. So they wrote 'Taxi' which was Steve's leaning and they wrote 'Capaldi's Café' which was Clive's leaning, and there was a track for Steve Lindsey and a track for that. It was a disparate record, a hard record to break, still not getting radio play – 'We're still not gonna play a group called Deaf School' – so we didn't have a lot of luck with that one.

But my great memory was of 'Capaldi's Café' having that thuggy chorus on it, and I'm singing on that. We had a sell-out concert at Leicester University and for one of the encores they did 'Capaldi's' and brought me up on stage. It was the one time, of all the gigs I've ever been to before and since, my only time on stage before a sell-out crowd. And I suddenly realised, which helped me in later life, the drug that's released from standing on stage. Particularly on the encores when they were going crazy. I said to Clive, I suddenly get why you do this!

Clive Langer's growing interest in the studio process made him, in effect, Rob's co-producer. It's curious how the experience had opposite effects on the two partners: for Clive it confirmed his eventual career path. For Rob, it was a sign that production would never be his calling in life. First Clive:

> Even though Rob Dickins was the producer, we were kind of doing it together. It wasn't showing off, it was about wanting to make this record. And I think I was allowed to do mostly what I wanted. I know it's rough, it's like demos, because I wasn't told it should have been cleaned up a bit. But I really like it now. Listening to it, it's kind of mad. And it's got 'Capaldi's' and 'Taxi' on it, so even though it's not a glossy album it's probably got two of the most important songs we do. And I love all that 'Hypertension' and 'Don't Stop the World', and trying to be punky yet melodic, and 'Friday on My Mind' [a 1966 pop hit by the Easybeats] is in there as well.

Max Ripple agrees: 'The second album was our reflection on the first one, an antithesis. Or it seemed to be, in that it had the hallmarks of something harsh, edgy, more real: "Wake up, we're not in 1940s Hollywood any more." But actually there's some quite camp things as well, so it's a very odd mixture.'

But Rob Dickins faced the problem of taking a multi-purpose cabaret troupe and turning them into a recognisable sonic identity. He was an outsider, but the insiders were hopelessly fragmented. 'It was almost an alpha male competitive thing,' he says.

Someone had to be in control because they disagreed on everything. Absolutely everything. And a couple of times I was close to a nervous breakdown, having to deal with these people not wanting to make the same record. You're trying to make something gel. What made them so unique and fun was also what made them not commercial.

It cured me of wanting to be a record producer, I know that. Later, when I A&R'd projects, dealt with producers and bands, I always had empathy with the producers. Because you're trying to make a record and they [the act] are almost trying to destroy a record. If you let the bass player do the mix the bass will be too loud, let the drummer do it the drums are too loud. It's the natural thing of me-me-me, you have to have an ego to be in a band. That's why a lot of good producers are calm: Chris Thomas, Glyn Johns, George Martin, there's a serenity about the great producers. You're either serene like they are or you're a bully like Guy Stevens, who would frighten you into it. And I was trying to do a bit of both. But you have to be one or the other.

'The second album was odd,' remembers Ian Ritchie. 'For the first one, we'd been together for quite a length of time, so we had a load of tunes and those were basically cherry-picked for the first album. The second album, Clive and Rob Dickins were in control much more. There was a lot of pressure for it to be new stuff, and we'd used the best of the old stuff for the first album. So I remember recording things like "Bad Habits", getting so far, then dropping some of the older songs, "Hot Jazz", getting into the recording then leaving those out. "Taxi" is very much the highlight from the second album.'

Many Deaf School fans would probably agree. And to this day, Enrico acknowledges its value in the stage set: 'The first time we played "Taxi", brand new, the roof came off, it was one of those songs. And we knew, Wow, the drama, the way the audience gets into every part of that song and knows it. It was really uplifting. "Taxi" is always the point in the set where nothing can go wrong afterwards. That's what we feel like, even if we've had to struggle with some new songs. You see that "Taxi" is next on the set-list: Oh, we're OK now! And it kind of rolls on from there, incredibly well.'

Steve Lindsey contributes 'Darling', an immaculate pop ballad. And Sam Davis, as well as co-writing the Dury-ish stomper 'Capaldi's Café' (named after a much-loved neighbourhood diner in Liverpool), had a big hand in 'Rock Ferry'. The title itself came from Enrico, inspired by a landing-point on the River Mersey's Wirral bank: 'I'd always loved the name Rock Ferry. Even Duffy has used it, hasn't she? [*Rockferry* was the Welsh singer's 2008 debut album; her father's family lived in the area.] So Rock Ferry for me was nothing to do with Bryan Ferry. It was just like Sandhills, a shitty place on the railway line from Maghull to Liverpool, but what a lovely name. Rock Ferry was another one of those for me. I had a couple of lines for it, and then Sam came in with "I'm going home to Rock

Ferr-ay, hand me my coat and my beret." I said, Oh, you write it, that's really good.'

For all the record's eventual diversity, the sleeve design reflects a harder outlook, in part a response to punk and also a simple desire to move on from *2nd Honeymoon*. 'That one was a complete sea-change,' confirms its designer Kevin Ward. 'I probably came up with that cover more in collaboration with Clive than any other member of the band. I wanted it to be very hard and graphic, Clive with his head in a pair of lift doors that were trying to shut. On the back I had this perverse idea that *Don't Stop the World* should actually be a shop. So we made a carrier bag. I can't explain my thinking in those days!'

With hindsight, Max Ripple questions even the album title. *'Don't Stop the World*? There's a question of whether you should ever do a negative statement. After the first album, which was warm and full-colour, this was black and white. "Stop the world" is negative, and "Don't stop the world" is doubly negative. And on the cover there's the pain of Clive being trapped in a lift, trapped in the punk era. I think we were feeling the cold wind of change around us. We had so many dimensions that we could have moved in various directions, but I think we were probably stampeded.'

Bette Bright's summary is perhaps even bleaker: 'Clive was very unhappy. All that energy, but there was all this stuff going on and he just wanted to be out there, playing his guitar. We were just so ill-timed. We'd done a load of recording for that second album and it was nowhere near as good as the first, it really was a rag-bag of styles. Then at the eleventh hour Clive just went, "Right! That's it!" And we re-did it really fast. You couldn't really do those songs live. We did a tour with that second album and it was just, Oh my God, half these songs were dreadful, and the saving grace was you'd end up doing "Final Act" and some of that song would get through to people.'

Don't Stop the World was released in March 1977, preceded in January by the single 'Taxi'. (Unfortunately for Deaf School's commercial momentum, but probably indicative of Warners' wavering faith, there was no second single.) This time around the *NME* devoted more space to their review, but its impulse was not encouragement. Their star punk journalist, Julie Burchill, called it 'Ten very clever pastiches and some neat tunes, but the last thing rock and roll needs at the moment.' In other words, Deaf School might be talented entertainers but the times demanded fierce sincerity. The band, she decided, inhabit 'an empty, elegant emporium of esoteric tack'.

As with the punk insurgency in general, the bigger old-school bands could weather such a drubbing. If you were Judas Priest or Genesis, your audience saw harsh reviews as the honourable scars of battle, the price of fighting the good fight. But Deaf School depended on the music press to reach the next level of their potential market. Reviewing had become a sort of blood sport, and Julie Burchill had fangs. Rock in 1977 was a cause, a movement. Art was judged according to its position, for or against, to the extent it might advance the revolution or hinder it.

All in all, it was a good time for Deaf School to leave the country.

SEVEN

America Was Our Hamburg

*Limousines to Los Angeles – Cowboy Boots and
Groupies – Goodbye Manhattan, Hello Birkenhead*

'A FTER WE'D DONE THE second album,' remembers Steve
Lindsey, 'we had an opportunity to tour America.
Derek Taylor loved the band and he just thought, "Let's
get Deaf School out to America and see what happens."
Back then record companies could think like that. They
could speculate. They can't do it now. It was a big tour,
seven weeks, and we did the length and breadth of the
place. We didn't visit Chicago or Detroit but did pretty
much every other major city.'

Punk rock was really an American invention. New
York's underground scene, in particular, had spawned the
Ramones, Television, Blondie, Talking Heads, Patti Smith
and more, all in a lineage of twisted garage bands that

included Andy Warhol's protégés the Velvet Underground. Malcolm McLaren himself learned the ropes through his pre-Pistols management of the New York Dolls. Having said that, visionaries in Manhattan, Detroit or Cleveland were still small fry in the wider context of the USA. The British mutation of punk, epitomised by the Sex Pistols, was yet to make any impression on the American mainstream.

Maybe the States might welcome Deaf School with no preconceptions? As Average says: 'It was a very confused time. We weren't the genuine article as far as punk was concerned in 1977. But when we went over to America we felt we were part of the avant-garde, taking punk to America.' Their itinerary would open in San Francisco on 10 May, and ended in Boston on 20 June, after some 30-odd dates that took in rock'n'roll landmarks like the Whisky a Go Go on LA's Sunset Strip and New York's scuzzy punk shrine CBGB. Along the way were encounters with the US heartland in cities such as Tucson, Denver, Dallas and Atlanta.

Their tour manager was Noel Monk, a practised hand who would soon perform the same service for the Sex Pistols, and went on to manage Van Halen. The road manager brought from Britain was Richard Boote, who compiled a souvenir dossier of the trip entitled *Wot We Did On Our Olidays: Deaf School In The Good Ole USA*. And from this document we see that the band left from Clive's dad's hotel on 6 May, in two Warner Brothers limousines, to catch the Heathrow Pan Am flight 121. At San Francisco, Pan Am staff were paging the tour party, under the impression they were deaf.

Asked, in *A Hard Day's Night*, how they found America,

a Beatle replies that they'd 'turned left at Greenland'. The truth was of course more complicated, and so it was for Deaf School. Ian Ritchie was enchanted:

> It was an amazing experience for me, particularly. I think the others were really looking forward to the American tour, and a lot of cultural things. A lot of those early songs had an American influence, from films and everything, and I had no interest. I wasn't struck about going to America, so I had a fantastic time because there was no expectation, and to me it was incredibly exciting. The first place we went to was San Francisco, we stayed in the Miyako, a Japanese-style hotel and everybody else was feeling vaguely disappointed that we weren't getting pancakes for breakfast or something, we were given miso soup. They had a preconception of what they wanted, and for me this was all interesting and different.

Deaf School were initially booked to support a bigger band, fronted by the Canadian drummer Corky Laing. Their first sound-check, at San Francisco's Old Waldorf, was severely curtailed by technicians setting up Laing's vast drum kit. 'For the first four or five nights,' remembers Ian, 'every gig, we were going down a storm and Corky was doing badly.

> He had a great band, but I remember doing the Whisky in LA, where you would get four sets: support band, main band, support band, main band. The club would fill when we'd play, then empty during Corky's set, fill again for our set, then empty. And Corky, who had been in Mountain, was saying

at the beginning of the tour, 'I'm not going to do any Mountain songs, just my own things', and as the days passed, more and more Mountain songs were creeping into the set. But it didn't make any difference. So then he pulled out. [Laing left the tour prior to a Denver gig on 24 May.] And about half the clubs cancelled the tour but half carried on. So it meant we went to places like Atlanta for four days and only did one gig.

Corky Laing, as noted, had made his reputation with the hard rock band Mountain. By 1972 he and his guitarist Leslie West were sufficiently famous to form a breakaway 'supergroup' with Cream's bassist Jack Bruce, called West, Bruce & Laing. But they never made much headway and Laing struck out on his own. Ironically, launching a new album with Brit-rockers Mick Ronson and Ian Hunter in 1978, he encountered much the same difficulties as Deaf School: 'This was the end of the '70s,' he later told *The Word* magazine, 'and who pops up but the fuckin' Cars. So basically Corky Laing and all his pals became irrelevant once the punkers started to come in and the record just went straight on to the shelf. The label didn't want to promote the '70s hierarchy at that point. We were done.'

✴✴✴

Evidenced by hundreds of Polaroid snaps in Deaf School's personal archives, the trip was a glorious opportunity to sample Touristville USA, the land of motels, souvenir cowboy hats and all-night hamburger joints. Tim Whittaker was especially smitten by that local delicacy the corn-dog. Bette Bright preferred the thrift shops of Texas, and bought vintage frocks by the trunkful. And there was the *Spinal Tap* side to it: 'Every town you went to,' says Frank, 'you had to go to the record store and do a promotion, meet-and-greet and so on. This was extraordinary for the band, and for me, to travel all expenses paid around America, hotels, aircraft...'

The great West Coast fleshpot of Los Angeles is by tradition a palace of excess for visiting British bands, and Deaf School had a whole four nights at its foremost shrine to decadence, the Whisky. By their own admission, however, Deaf School were never great groupie-magnets. Mr Average suggests that having a girl singer was something to do with it, and their arty image may have suggested they were above that sort of thing. (The road crew, he couldn't help noticing, had no such problems.) Personally he found it all quite disappointing, having thought that was half the point of being in a band.

Clive: 'America, to me... I was single. We weren't a rock band chasing the chicks, I was never like that. But going to America, we'd play the Whisky in LA, then go to a club, some girls would invite us. It was the beginning of punk, you'd be talking to a girl and you'd feel a hand on your thigh, and that was something completely new to me. I wasn't a big shagger, but it was a new experience.'

Max Ripple accepts the Spinal Tappish aspects of a US tour, but also rues the personal cost to his marriage: 'Personally it was always quite painful being away from home, being on the road, having children. I mean, I should never have done it, looking back. That was a disaster, really, in terms of marriage. It might have broken up anyway. But you did an hour of the gig every night and then the whole routine of being on the road is not always as glamorous as it seems. It's kind of a strange life.

'There was a roadie, who used to come up to you and say, "Fucking-A, man! Fucking-A." Which he thought was very English, somehow. We had a person from Warner Brothers who kept trying to get us to throw TVs out of the window. I do re-runs of it now where we would be geriatrically struggling to get the plasma screen off the wall, asking for help.' (Ken Testi, too involved with Eric's Club to join the tour, observes that Max is prone to some rock'n'roll madness. He says the Reverend once claimed to have thrown a TV out of the window, but the band were in fact on the ground floor – and he had thoughtfully placed it on a hedge.)

There was some excitement at the Sheraton Hotel, however, where Deaf School were introduced to Elton John, and saw Telly 'Kojak' Savalas in the swimming pool. There were visits to Disneyland and to the Warner HQ in Burbank (sometimes called 'the Rabbit Hutch' for its Bugs Bunny connection). Warner executives, including Derek, came to watch the band play, a rare chance to assess this eccentric investment at close range. *Sounds*' Barbara Charone was again on hand, writing up the shows with unabashed enthusiasm ('Deaf School Wow The USA – Barbara Charone Waxes Lyrical').

Steve Lindsey's favourite moment came one night after a Whisky show, when Derek Taylor brought along his friend Harry Nilsson. 'When I wrote "Final Act",' says Average, 'mucking around with these chords, I thought, "This sounds a bit Harry Nilsson-ish." And then we played the Whisky, and afterwards went to Derek's suite at the Beverly Hills Hotel. So there was a few of us in a circle and Harry Nilsson was ordering room service, lovely guy, and was saying "I really enjoyed it, thanks, I particularly liked 'Final Act', the song that the girl sang at the end." Wonderful! I didn't say, That was *my* song! I just... glowed.'

Moving on to Atlanta, on 8 June they were introduced by Noel Monk to a US producer, Sonny Limbo: 'I like what you're doing, come to my home studio,' he said to them, and an attempt was duly made on their new song 'I Wanna be Your Boy'. 'It didn't work,' notes Max, 'perhaps predictably, because he was used to dealing with real musicians.' There was another disappointment on 11 June, according to Richard Boote's diary. Eric/Sam was upset to hear from Warners that 'Capaldi's Café' would not be released as a single. True, he'd been the main vocalist for a change, but he was surely correct in spotting a lost opportunity.

The tour's penultimate city was New York, for three nights (and six shows) at the renowned CBGB club. 'We had done a kind of carefully worked-out tour,' says Max, 'from the West Coast right the way through to New York. That was presumably Derek's standard sample tour, where you start off with the gay scene in San Francisco and if they like you then you're ahead of the game. Then we went through Tucson and eventually to Denver. And if they like you in Denver, release it immediately! Then you get to New York, and I don't think it's exactly an American town, but that was the way to find out what a band was going to be.'

If Deaf School were essentially a Limey curiosity elsewhere in the States, though warmly received, there seemed a decent chance of being fully understood at CBGB. This after all was the venue which had nurtured

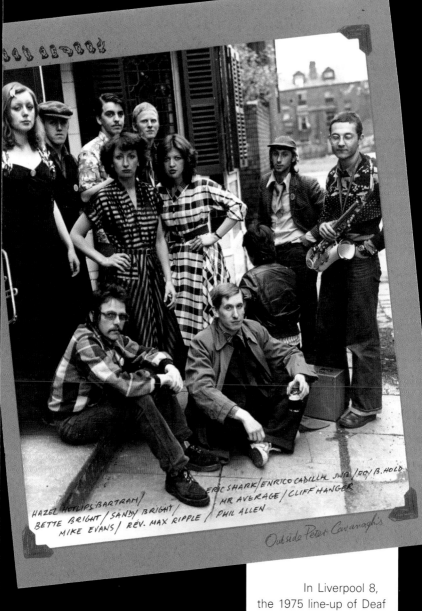

HAZEL HOTLIPS BARTRAM /
BETTE BRIGHT / SANDY BRIGHT /
MIKE EVANS / REV. MAX RIPPLE /

ERIC SHARK / ENRICO CADILLAC JNR. / RON B. HOLD
MR AVERAGE / CLIFF HANGER
PHIL ALLEN

Outside Peter Cavanagh's

In Liverpool 8, the 1975 line-up of Deaf School that won the Melody Maker contest. Roadie Phil sits in for missing drummer Tim.

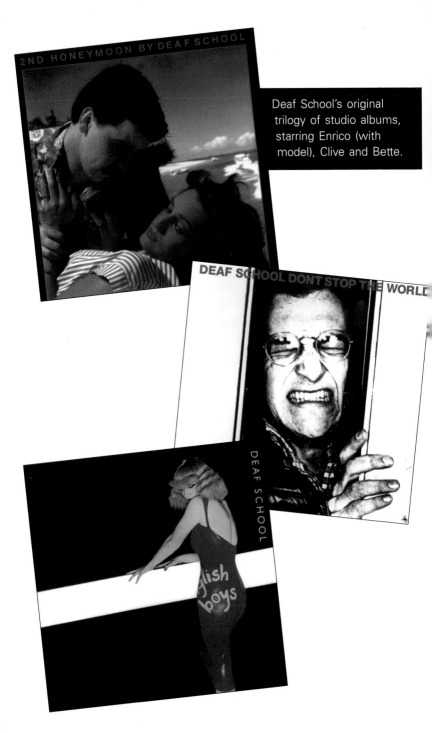

Deaf School's original trilogy of studio albums, starring Enrico (with model), Clive and Bette.

TIMOTHY WHITTAKER
RIC SHARK   FRANK AVERAGE   BETTE BRIGHT   ENRICO CADILLAC JNR   IAN RITCHIE   REV MAX RIPPLE

DEAF SCHOOL   CLIFF LANGER

Going up… or down? The
1977 line-up that signed
to Warner Brothers.

'America was our Hamburg': Eric, Tim and Enrico in Polaroids from the US tour, 1977.

At the shrines of LA rock, the Whisky club and Tower Records: Ian, Frank Silver (in black) and Max. Below: US promo badge.

Fresh from America, Deaf School play York University, October 1977. All photos by Neville Astley.

Left: the Steve Hardstaff flyer for Deaf School's residency in 1975. Below: Enrico is joined by Kevin Rowland and Suggs at Steve 'Average' Lindsey's birthday gig, 2005. Photo by Paul Terence Madden.

US punk. And where London punk was fast becoming a self-parodic formula, New York retained enough of its arty open-mindedness to embrace some real diversity. Clive Langer:

> When we played CBGBs with the Shirts, they were quite big in America at that time, but I think we were more interesting. We were as interesting as Blondie; probably not as interesting as Television, because we weren't at that level of musicality. But we were an interesting phenomenon. And if they'd just left us there in New York, just let us sit there for three or four weeks instead of 'You do two shows and you're out', we probably could have happened. We'd do one night in Texas and they'd ask us if wanted to do a second night. Places like Austin were rock, bluesy places, but they were moving forward and they really appreciated something different. So when we played in Houston or wherever, we got a great reaction. We got a great reaction everywhere. Steve was such a great showman. I mean, we were 'weird' to them, but people liked the weirdness.

The long march across America was nearly over and Deaf School had toughened up. They were almost becoming the punk band that Clive dreamed of playing in. 'We wrecked CBGB's,' says Ian. 'I recall Steve Lindsey taking his bass and stabbing it into the ceiling, and Enrico jumping on tables and knocking people's drinks off. It was just about being outrageous, punky in that way.' The respected critic Robert Palmer, writing in the *New York Times*, liked what he saw: while Deaf School 'seemed to be courting a punk image', they were also 'wildly eclectic', veering from

1960s British Invasion pop to hard rock to European café music, amounting to a 'semi-satirical punk Dada revue... promisingly bizarre'.

By the final date, at Boston's Jazz Workshop, a second set became so hyper-energetic that Enrico punched through the ceiling with his fist. As Frank Silver says: 'The Americans did not know what to make of this look. It wasn't what they were expecting. They thought we might be like the Tubes. Deaf School had been sold as an art school band but they ended up being a punk band.'

'The gigs were great,' says Ian Ritchie, 'but we were making this change into another band. The aggressive part was coming into play and I could never hear what I was playing. The band were getting louder and louder. Musically that was the beginning of the end for me. So on the one hand the experience was fantastic, but musically it wasn't so good. I think Clive would probably disagree.' Indeed he does:

> The most exciting thing is playing in a band. America was just amazing, two shows a night, 17 shows, and we got really good. That was like our Hamburg. Before we went, we'd do a show and you wouldn't know if it was going to be good or bad. When we came back, we knew all the shows were going to be good. And even if they weren't amazing, the professionalism now kicked in.
>
> It was the best time of my life. Being in America. Just the freedom, getting confident, not having to deal with the punk thing, which we'd just left behind. Here, *we* were the new thing, like we'd been before. Then you got back to Liverpool and it was June 1977, and punk was commercial by then.

God knows what that first tour must have cost Warners. We were flown internally 17 times, and we had two station wagons waiting for us all the while. The problem was that we were such a big band, numerically. If we'd been a four piece they could have stuck us in a bus, but being an eight-piece we'd need two buses or a coach. But the great thing was we'd play somewhere and we'd have a day off the next night and the promoter loved us, so we'd say 'Well, we'll do another gig for you tomorrow night, if you like, cos we're in town.' So while we were going along we were gaining a lot of friends.

Richard Boote computed they had played precisely 39 sets, in 16 venues. A little tired, Deaf School left the USA on 23 June, flying to Heathrow for a connecting flight to Liverpool Speke Airport. Back in the States, Warners compiled the first two British albums into a double-vinyl version for the American market. 'We'd toured at vast expense,' concludes Frank Silver. 'And Warners paid for all that investment in the hope that it would take off. Unfortunately it never did.'

***

America, to use Clive's analogy, may well have been Deaf School's Hamburg. Unfortunately, whereas the Beatles' tough apprenticeship in Germany came usefully early, setting them up for all that followed, Deaf School's own particular boot-camp happened a little too late in their career trajectory. Bette sums it up: 'Punk came along and we were broadsided, and then we were on this tour of America, which was crazy, but it was good experience for sure. We were doing two shows a night and we got really tight. But that was really the end of Deaf School. Clive had just had enough. He wanted to be off in a punk band.'

That was not the absolute end of Deaf School's American adventures, however. About a month later, following a homecoming show at Eric's and a few other gigs, they were flown back to New York for a cable TV appearance at the chic cabaret club Reno Sweeney's. So chic was it that even the celebrity author Truman Capote was around. Deaf School's vintage aspect should have played well in the joint's retro-glam atmosphere, but as Clive recalls, 'It was a complete disaster. We were jet-lagged, we were flown in and out, they put us in this little club with an invited audience. Warners were filming another band as well, so we didn't get on until 11 or 12, and we'd been drinking since about 6.'

Average, to be fair, thinks the greater problem was an outbreak of flu in the ranks. 'I had to go to a doctor's surgery. About five of us went to have our nasal passages drained, it was horrible.' The footage confirms his voice, on 'Darling', as shot to pieces, but there is a brittle, ska-calypso reading of 'Nearly Moonlit Night Motel' and a storming, hardcore version of 'Capaldi's Café'.

'Steve and Anne were together,' adds Clive, 'but a bit volatile. *So*, when we went on, she hit him over the head with a recorder at some point. He got on stage, went to grab the mic and missed, and went sliding off at the other end. It was our one shot, as well, we'd been flown to New York to do this video and it was a mess. Anyway, they kept it and it's always being shown. Maybe it's interesting but it's mad. But it just wasn't the professional video they thought they were going to get from us, to break Deaf School.'

Derek Taylor kept the faith, however, and recorded a wry voiceover to introduce Warners' promo film of the band:

> Deaf School is not an ordinary rock and roll band. A few years ago, they were a mixed bunch of art students in Liverpool, in England, who came together to play for the *Melody Maker* new bands competition in London, and won. Derek Taylor, the former Beatles press officer, now a vice-president of Warner Brothers, saw them and quickly signed them.

And this last statement is a little embarrassing because I do seem to *be* Derek Taylor. But someone has to say these things and I do at least mean it. The band is made up of eight distinct and distinctive characters who are playing music and also playing parts on stage. They have two albums out on Warner Brothers, a third to be released in 1978.

They learned a lot from old Hollywood movies. Now here on the front line we have Enrico Cadillac Jnr, a visual cross between Clark Gable and Lon Chaney Jnr. Eric Shark, also a vocalist, who might have wandered in from a Raymond Chandler novel. Bette Bright, also a vocalist, in transition from being Rita Hayworth to becoming a lady with a past. On keyboards the Reverend Max Ripple, a debauched English parish priest, in real life formerly a teacher in art school. On bass, the youngest member of the band, Frankie Average, who never forgot his Liverpool roots, in his Cardin Beatles suit. On sax Ian Ritchie, who would have been playing jazz in the 50s but is far too young. On drums Tim Whittaker, personally favouring black leather jackets and bleached blond hair. On guitar, Cliff or Clive Langer with glasses and a large brain.

They sing nice songs about cocktails at 8, about suicide, and about hangovers and about life in all its infinite variety. And really, it's good old rock and roll. And now, Deaf School…

Those were the excitements of America, but now it was back to the grind of ordinary British touring. After their encounter with Manhattan's fashionable *demi-monde* in Reno Sweeney's, it's poignant that the next Deaf School gig was at a club called Mr Digby's in Birkenhead. That's show business.

* * *

But at least Merseyside remained a fortress of Deaf School loyalism. The band's appeal transcended its art school origins: in these working-class bastions Deaf School really were a People's Band. Nicky Allt, nowadays a well-established playwright, remembers the atmosphere among his peer group of the time:

> Young, unemployed rag-arse kids in the late '70s, myself, my small band of Liverpool and Everton supporting mates… We all thought we were the Boys. The Football Lads. The Bee's Knees! Our gang dressed differently, we acted differently at all costs, and we had our hard-case walks and talks.
>
> We also had our bands. Yes, we loved David Bowie,

the Jam and the Clash like other kids in other places, but 'our band' was Deaf School. It was Deaf School songs we sang on trains to away games. An 18-year-old Scouse lad attempting to sing 'Room Service' to an audience of 20, on an early morning inter-city train to London Euston, really is a bit eccentric.

Like us, Deaf School were always trying to be different. When Enrico Cadillac wore his Hawaiian shirt we started wearing them too. Late '77, dressed in Adidas Samba, Fred Perry T-shirts and tight-leg Levi jeans we'd been taunted at Leeds United's Elland Road ground as 'just a bunch of queers!' We lapped it up. Where others felt intimidated by the abuse, we felt lifted, as though we were the all-travelling Deaf School for the day. In Liverpool, not even Bowie had that aura at the time.

Deaf School were a madly eccentric bunch who made, it seemed, music to suit themselves. We acted that way daily and it seemed, in our teen-logic, like they were the musical extension of us.

When Bette sang 'Final Act', ending a Saturday night show not long after that Leeds game, I dived on stage to nab a kiss and hog a microphone, and amazingly – she let me join in. OK, with one eye on the bouncers, it was only for 20 seconds or so, but, by God Bette girl, if you're reading this, I walked about like God's gift the whole of the following week. And no away supporter was gonna dampen my cocky swagger for the rest of that football season. After a hug and a kiss from Bette Bright I was suffering from a bad case of what we used to call 'five-foot-eight going on seven-foot-two'.

We wanted to follow Deaf School, we wanted to be in Deaf School, and we wanted the world to know about Deaf School. That the whole world didn't remained a complete mystery to all of us.

We should not overlook the glamour of Bette Bright in explaining Deaf School's appeal: moreover, she wasn't pleading for these boys' attention, she commanded it. A few years later in the *NME* I asked her about sex symbol status: 'Well it kinda gets on my nerves. Most blokes are pretty sexual on stage and they don't get attacked for it. But if you're a woman then it becomes the obvious thing for people to say about you.'

Other fans at that time included a local schoolboy Guy Chambers, who would be a future member of World Party and probably best-known as songwriting partner of Robbie Williams. And there is the tale of an Eric's punk, Kevin, who was expelled from school on the verge of his GCEs. After parental pleading he was allowed back to take the lesser CSEs. Before the English exam he revealed to a friend his plan to fill the exam paper with pop lyrics of the day. The friend was duly struck by this scheme and filled his own paper with 10cc's 'I'm Not in Love'. Not surprisingly he failed. But Kevin, more smartly, opted for 'Don't Stop the World' and 'Rock Ferry', achieving the grade 1 pass that was equivalent to a GCE.

We could almost encapsulate Deaf School's legacy to Liverpool in three words: Big In Japan. Essentially a Deaf School offshoot, this irregular combo was not only the Eric's house band, but the academy for an entire new wave of musicians. Once, they had gone to watch Deaf School and been inspired; now they joined Big In Japan and found themselves on stage. As a *Melody Maker* report would put it, five years later: 'Deaf School, led by Clive Langer, loaded and cocked the rifle, but it was Big In Japan who pulled the trigger.'

Enrico's younger brother Phil Allen explains that he was roadie-ing for Deaf School, and Kevin Ward was still doing the lights, but neither was allowed a work visa for the US tour. At Clive's suggestion they formed a scratch band to pass the time in Deaf School's absence, together with Bill Drummond, the stage-builder from the Everyman and O'Halligan's. Roger Eagle offered rehearsal space at Eric's, and revelled in the chaotic punk noise they created. On vocals they acquired Jayne Casey, the shaven-headed queen of a Mathew Street art-terror gang that sprang from her stall in Aunt Twacky's and came to embody the Eric's ethos. Phil Allen:

> Steve was sending me postcards from the States, and one said, 'We just did a terrible gig in Atlanta, but we got some news that we're big in Japan.' The LP was selling well there. A few days later me and Bill and Kevin were sitting in the caff trying to think of a name and I said, Why don't we just go on and say, 'You've never heard of us but we're big in Japan.' And that was it.
>
> By the time Deaf School got back from the States we had Jayne in the band, we played to Clive at Eric's one afternoon and he was flabbergasted that we'd actually done it. I think he was a little bit jealous as well. At that time he was feeling a bit jaded. Bill Drummond went on holiday for a couple of weeks and Clive joined the band when Bill was away. And we had a recording session, doing 'Big In Japan', and we did a little tour. When Bill came back I don't think

Clive wanted to leave, but he had commitments to Deaf School.

'Clive wanted to do stuff like we were doing,' adds Kevin Ward. 'What had happened in the British music industry was like a seismic change. And it happened so quickly. And I think Clive wanted to be part of that.' 'I was hanging out more with Big In Japan than I was with Deaf School,' Clive remembers of this time, 'because Steve was with Anne. Socially I'd hang out with Steve when he was single, otherwise I'd hang out with his brother and Kevin and all the people at Eric's. I'd be at Roger's at night, listening to the singles that he'd spent all his money on, all his profit from that weekend at Eric's! And fall asleep on his stinky old bed.'

Big In Japan had Eric's to play in, Deaf School's gear to play with and the pick of any support slot they fancied. Steve Hardstaff provided artwork. New musicians joined including Holly Johnson (before Frankie Goes To Hollywood), Ian Broudie (before the Lightning Seeds), Budgie (before Siouxsie & the Banshees) and Dave Balfe (before The Teardrop Explodes). Record companies showed interest and, incongruously, Big In Japan were given a session at the Moody Blues' huge Threshold studio in London. And then Rob Dickins became involved:

I became a bit of a legend in Liverpool because I'd produced Deaf School. Clive formed Big In Japan and then because of Deaf School he left it. So Bill [Drummond] came to see me and said, 'We love the stuff you do with Deaf School, will you produce Big In Japan?' So I did 'Society for Cutting Up Men' and 'Suicide A Go Go', with Alan Winstanley at TW in

Fulham. This was even before Madness. So by virtue of that I met Bill, Dave (Balfe), Holly Johnson who was 17, Jayne Casey, Kevin Ward, Budgie and Ian Broudie. It was extraordinary. At the time they were just these kids from Liverpool, far more Liverpudlian than Deaf School, actually.

Holly Johnson had discovered Deaf School in his early teens through one of their album adverts in *Melody Maker*. He told the *Guardian* in 2011 that he conceived 'a sort of crush on their singers Bette Bright and Enrico Cadillac, both of whom wore eyeshadow'. Too young to see them play, he nevertheless gloried in the fact they were local and offered a replacement for the Beatles. Immersing himself in the first two albums, 'What a Way to End it All' became for him a musical 'benchmark'. He finally met them at Eric's, as Big In Japan rehearsed with Deaf School's equipment.

At this point, in 1977, Deaf School were scarcely a 'Liverpool band' any more, but global artists. 'They were the absent leaders of this scene,' wrote Holly for the Deaf School website, 'off on tour or making another record. It was Anne [Bette Bright] who advised me to join the Performing Rights Society as a songwriter, always looking fabulous in a Swanky Modes dress or swanning down Bold Street in a pink and blue Seditionaries mohair sweater.'

Created by Clive, christened by Steve, Big In Japan were the next stage in Liverpool's renaissance. On 3 May 1977, just as Deaf School were touching down in San Francisco, the Clash played a gig at Eric's that seemed to galvanise the junior band (though Jayne never shared the boys' enthusiasm). This was the night that Liverpool really 'got' punk rock. The Sex Pistols' show at Eric's the previous

October had attracted fewer than 50 people. (And Colin Fallows, a Deaf School follower at the time, recalls the London act were greeted as a sort of comic turn.) Big In Japan were never built to last, however, and they barely survived into 1978. But they had certainly left their mark.

Ken Testi parted ways with Roger Eagle and Pete Fulwell, and Eric's itself would close down in 1980, beset by creditors, police attention and the stark lack of punters on midweek evenings when no big names were appearing. Roger Eagle went on to various other ventures, though nothing matched the profile of Eric's. After a period of ill-health he died in 1999. But the Eric's generation of bands swept to national fame. Bill Drummond and Dave Balfe formed their Zoo label, a launch platform for Echo & the Bunnymen, The Teardrop Explodes and the Wild Swans. (Drummond, of course, had a whole subsequent career with the KLF and others.) About the same time came Orchestral Manoeuvres In The Dark, Pete Wylie's Wah! Heat (and its successors) and Pete Burns, another of Mathew Street's wild outsiders, who founded Dead or Alive.

* * *

Don't Stop the World had plainly failed to open new doors for Deaf School. There was nothing for it, now, but to head for the open road and slog it out.

As Steve Allen observed of South Wales and Birmingham, there were definite pockets of Deaf School support outside Liverpool. Across the Pennines, Neville Astley was a student who saw the band on that 1975 *Melody Maker* cover: 'I thought, Wow, what an interesting looking group of people. Then I saw them a few times at college gigs in Leeds and York. I liked them in the way I liked bands like Alex Harvey who were theatrical, but not just cabaret. You believed in them as a proper band as well as being that visual feast. Then one night I took my camera along because I knew how amazing they were to watch.'

Astley's camera has seen action at many Deaf School gigs since then, as well as supplying a band portrait for the *Enrico & Bette* CD. (He is probably better known, though, as a co-creator of the phenomenally popular children's animation *Peppa Pig*.) What struck him was Deaf School's ability to summon forth a hidden tribe of like-minded souls: 'It was interesting that suddenly they dragged out all the more artistic people in York, and they gravitated towards this gig. Looking through some of the pictures recently, I noticed in the crowd shots so many people who were known in York for their artistic flamboyance. It touched a nerve on so many levels.'

But tensions were surfacing. Dan Silver, helping his brother Frank with Deaf School's admin, typed a note to all personnel: 'Frank advises that on the forthcoming tour, *everyone* must take great care that they have enough sleep and cat sufficient *decent* food to ensure that the strains of travelling are not exacerbated by being irritable and tired through lack of sleep, and weary because of lack of good food.'

Back in April, just before the US tour, Max Ripple had actually written a letter of resignation:

Dear Deaf School,
    You may have heard the rumour that I am 'leaving' the band: to put your mind at rest and clarify the position, here are some points to ponder... pause for

pissed version of You've Lost That Loving Feeling (any key you like, so long as it's F# or G.)

1. I am over 16
2. I cannot, nor ever could, play keyboards half as well as your next keyboard player.
3. Despite all my vigilance and care, spiritual values within the band have declined over the last 3 years.
4. I have been increasingly aware of my inability to develop musically alongside the band.
5. You have been even more aware of this than I have.
6. Mike Evans could have been wrong when he said that getting a big PA and taking itself seriously could be the two downfalls of Deaf School.
7. I don't want to be the van's mascot.
8. Deaf has more chance of making it now than it ever did (despite popular opinion).
9. I am tired of having to wear denim and a floppy leather hat on stage.
10. I once wrote a good Deaf School song. If I could remember how it went I would write it again.

This resignation is negotiable ie become valid either before or after the forthcoming US tour (whichever is more convenient to Deaf School).

Yours sincerely,

Max Ripple

Though elegant in its self-deprecation, Max's letter does hint at various anxieties: he expected he might be replaced by Clive's schoolfriend Ben Barson; his fear of the 'denim and floppy leather hat' was code for an aversion to standard rock dramatics; and he no longer understood his role in this art school prank that had turned horribly serious. How did the band respond to the Reverend's *cri-de-coeur*? 'We laughed our heads off,' says Steve. 'It was so well-written. But we ignored it.'

Before he gave up his teaching work, Sam Davis had also been feeling the strain: 'We were on the front page of the *Melody Maker*, it was exciting. It got quite serious after that. Once we got a contract we had to do an album. At the time I was teaching at Netherley Comp and we were doing our first tour of Britain. So I'd get into work and have to say to my Head of Department, Look, Terry, I've got to be in Middlesbrough at 6 o'clock. He was great, he'd say "All right, we'll cover for you." I used to bunk off like the kids did, to go to these gigs and I'd turn up wrecked the next day cos I had to drive back through the night.'

Average, who at least got to complete his three-year course at Liverpool, acknowledges the toll his double life was taking:

> It was a real strain towards the end. In '75 we signed our record and publishing deals. Clive was soon well out of college, I was in college in all but body. But I clung on and finished the course, just about. I did a final show, and just wish I could have included Deaf School's first album and a list of all the gigs I'd done! I know we did two national tours before I finished art college. I needed to hand in one piece of written work and I didn't do it; Deaf School had become the preoccupation of my life.

> I remember sitting in the back of the van, we travelled up and down the country, we gigged a *huge* amount over the years, and I was thinking, This isn't pleasant, but I'm paying my dues.

I also remember us going into a pub in Liverpool and it was, 'Oh you've changed since you got that record deal.' 'No we haven't!' but I think we probably did. It's funny thinking back, the way that we'd be on the tour bus going from gig to gig and Steve would be doing his Scouse knockabout humour, but as we got closer to the stage time and he got changed into his Enrico gear, he actually would take on... you couldn't talk to him like Steve.

And towards the end, when we had the pressure of not having the success and knew our days were numbered, this quite unpleasant character would materialise, quite aggressive because of the punk influence that fed into the persona. It was weird, as the pencil moustache would go on and the eye make-up, that you couldn't speak to him as Steve Allen. It was quite frightening.

Max Ripple: 'I think there was a misgiving with people moving in different directions, as you find when there's a lack of momentum in the commercial side. And everybody had their own views, it was a big band. So you had the spectre of selling out or giving in to try and make things harmonious.'

It was unlucky for Deaf School that Derek Taylor, their record company mentor, now moved to a new role at Warners in Los Angeles. 'They got this other guy in,' remembered Sam, 'called John Fruin. And that was the start of the end really. The other thing that happened was the Head of A&R was Dave Dee, from Dave Dee, Dozy, Beaky, Mick & Titch and we couldn't give him much credibility, so our relationship with Warners was a bit more strained. Rob Dickins was Head of Publishing and he was always a friend but there was only so much that he could do.'

Ironically Derek was almost the man who signed both Deaf School *and* the Sex Pistols. 'In 1977,' he told me, 'after they left EMI and A&M a call came through to WEA as we'd just become. It was an early John Fruin meeting [he being the new MD of WEA]. I'd become Deputy MD of the new three-part group rather than MD of Warners alone, but I still had the lingering feeling that I had ultimate power. A call came through saying: "It's the manager of the Sex Pistols, Do we want them?" And I said "Yes!" And Fruin on my right said "No." So we didn't get them.' (By a further irony, the label that did succeed in nabbing the Pistols was Richard Branson's Virgin, narrowly pipped by Derek for Deaf School.)

Bette Bright: 'He was the first person I saw taking cocaine, Derek Taylor. I suppose the industry was changing, and the allure of having him there, because of who he was, was fading. But he was a gentleman. It was that time when there were a few decent people in the music business, before it all changed. We struck a chord with him and were lucky to have known him, for sure.'

Max Ripple: 'Derek. Such a lovely guy. And I think he saw both sides in us. He said once, "OK lads, which way do you want to go? If you want to do the kind of *Dad's Army*, I've got contacts in TV and I can get you into the theatre side of things if you want to develop that. Otherwise," – obviously the Byrds and the Beatles and all that background he had – "you can go whichever way you want."'

Clive: 'I don't think Warners the company had a clue what we were all about. We had to keep telling them what we should sound like, what the covers should be. And Derek got it, but he was still harking back to his mates in Monty Python. He didn't understand punk, really. By the last album I had to explain to him that I'd rather be a roadie for the Clash than be in this band. I felt I couldn't express myself through Deaf School. The band seemed to be clinging on to what we were when we started. I wanted to embrace punk and go beyond.'

Enrico: 'Derek wanted to do what he loved doing, which was work with George Melly. He wanted to do that lovely album *A Nightingale Sang in Berkeley Square*, with John LeMesurier. And why not, they were better records than a lot of the others that he did. That album he did with Harry Nilsson, *A Little Touch of Schmilsson in the Night*, that was brilliant. I don't think he was wrong, he was actually in the right time of his life to do those good projects and make them work. It was Derek who turned us on to *Banana Blush*, John Betjeman's record, he was involved with that too.'

Derek Taylor would eventually leave Warners in 1978, the same year as Deaf School, and the two departures were not entirely coincidental. It's a common problem for bands that their early champions move on or lose influence. Transferred to America, Derek's disillusionment had deepened:

> I wasn't interested in the music that much any more. I was then in Hollywood, a very structured situation with a massive budget. I began to dread people coming in with tapes under their arms and saying, 'D'you wanna hear the guy's new album?' Because I didn't. I wanted to hear George Formby. I'd have tapes from long ago in my desk. It was a

very alienating job by now, strictly business. But we did get the Sex Pistols for America. We had them on Warners in Burbank, and I worked closely with McLaren. I had the advertising, merchandising and marketing, as Director of Creative Services.

His last project for Warners was the Rutles, the consummate Beatle parodists born out of the Bonzos and Monty Python: 'After that I realised that was more or less it: I'd done the Beatles at the beginning and the Rutles at the end. Out!' Going into semi-retirement, Derek wrote his memoirs and assisted on various projects; he wrote some things for me when I launched *Mojo* magazine, and went back to Apple to work on the Beatles' massive *Anthology* project, where I met him for the final time. He died of cancer in 1997.

And Deaf School? For them, the moment of crisis was at hand.

EIGHT

'Sound of Rock
Fades for Deaf School'

*English Boys/Working Girls – Last Drink in
the Last Chance Saloon – The Final Act*

'THE SECOND RECORD DIDN'T change the world over there,'
Mr Average concedes. 'But when we got back from
America, Warners said, "OK, there's enough of a reason
to do a third album." They weren't pulling the plug. But it
was make-or-break time.' 'The other dimension,' adds Max
Ripple, 'is the pressure the record company puts on. If you
don't get anything on the first album then you won't do a
second one; if you do the second one, you either continue
on your upward path or else you really have to do your
last-ditch effort on the third.'

The pressing question became, Who will produce? Rob
Dickins: 'Again we started doing new demos down in TW
with Alan Winstanley. But I clearly was not the producer

that was going to give them a hit record. I'd had two albums' go at it, and completely realised this myself. So we thought about who would, and Mutt Lange at the time was producing hits, interesting records. It was decided they would move forward into working with Mutt.'

Average elaborates: 'It was, "Let's get a proper producer on board," and that's where Mutt Lange was brought in. He'd had a significant amount of success with the Boomtown Rats. So I think Warner Brothers said, "Ah, Boomtown Rats. Deaf School." They equated us. Mutt Lange was seen as a growing name, and therefore not as expensive as a real name, but also a safe pair of hands. And as we'd made some mark on America, he was seen as someone who'd know how to put an American twist on it.'

But a couple of other names were in contention. Clive admired the unobtrusive style of Chris Thomas, who had produced both Roxy Music and the Sex Pistols. But Roxy comparisons were something Deaf School needed to escape. (For that reason, as well as an aversion to second billing, they turned down a chance to support the band on tour.) And then there was the champion of no-frills pub rock – now a recognised punk/new wave producer, too – Nick Lowe.

'We went to see Nick about producing the third album,' says Clive, 'but it was the morning after Elvis Presley had died. I don't think he'd slept. There was a lot of drinking, obviously... My ideal would have been that Nick Lowe did the album, but it didn't happen. So we got Mutt Lange, who was the commercial side of Nick Lowe and we ended up with a funny-sounding album. It's got a funny sound to it.'

Robert John Lange, to use his official billing, was

destined to become one of the world's most successful producers of beefed-up, radio-friendly rock, boosting the fortunes of acts such as AC/DC, Def Leppard and his wife of several years, Shania Twain. In late 1977, however, he was just an up-and-coming talent whose credits included Graham Parker, the Motors, Liverpool's own Supercharge and the first Boomtown Rats album, which was home to their early hit singles 'Lookin' After No 1' and 'Mary of the Fourth Form'. 'He wasn't hugely busy then,' says Frank Silver, 'but he was an extraordinarily gifted producer, very hard-working.'

Time was booked over the Christmas period at the residential Rockfield Studios in Monmouth, South Wales. Queen's 'Bohemian Rhapsody' was the biggest of many hits recorded there, a testament to British art-rock and its glorious disregard for self-restraint. But Deaf School were put on a somewhat tighter leash. There was a natural temptation to follow any formula that seemed to be working for the Boomtown Rats: one track, 'Refugee', is brazenly similar. Elsewhere, the band's inclination to rock out is held in check by a brittle, new wave style that zips along but leaves no space for surprises.

A few songs, like 'Morning After', are drawn from memories of America ('There were a lot of morning afters on that tour,' says Steve). 'Working Girls' began life as 'Polish Hills', with a melodic nod to Clive's family ancestry. But, tellingly, it was one more song that Steve could not develop a lyrical feel for, and passed along to Eric Shark. Sam Davis would end up with four co-writes here, against Steve Allen's seven, a shift that gives the record a touch too much of the yob-Cockney vocals borrowed from Ian Dury. Steve Lindsey's 'All Queued Up' received a blistering vocal from Bette. 'I thought it was a potential single,' he says. 'So I was disappointed when Clive and the band said, "We've got to do this faster." It was because of the punk thing, and it got out of control. I remember a couple of years later, Enrico played that single at the wrong speed, at 33 not 45, and he said, "You know, it sounds better like that!" Timing is everything, and punk undermined a lot of what we were trying to do.' (The track was actually pressed up as a single but replaced at the last minute with 'Thunder and Lightning'.)

In Ian Ritchie's view, the album's whole identity was a result of their experiences in America:

> We'd gone to the States as a theatre-rock group, but when we arrived there, we metamorphosed to being a punk group, and the third album was basically a reaction against the climate that we were now old hat.
>
> Our first two albums hadn't been very successful anyway, so we had to do something different. All the songs that were written for the third album were written either during the American tour or as a reaction to that tour. We brought in Mutt Lange with the idea that he had some kind of punk credibility, which is slightly laughable but it must have seemed that way at the time. So we went up to Rockfield and basically made the album. Which was fascinating.
>
> And Mutt is a proper record producer. I think Muff Winwood was as well, but unfortunately we didn't really give him a chance. Whereas with Mutt we'd do pretty much whatever he wanted, Clive included. So Mutt basically made a Mutt Lange record, with loads of multi-tracking. On that album we didn't have the strength of songs of even the

second album, I don't think. And we weren't a punk band. I think I was under-used, I think Max was under-used, and the singers were forced into singing in that aggressive punky style. So to me that album is the least successful of them. A couple of nice things on it but that's not Deaf School for me.

And it was reflected in the gigs. We became much more like a rock band, which to me was a backward step, so it was becoming less interesting to a lot of members of the group. Once we got to the third album I think Clive wanted the band to be the Clash, he would have preferred that to Deaf School. The aspects of the band which I really loved, the cabaret theatrical aspects, I think to this day are the things which save us on stage, when things go wrong, and we're playing rather badly. If we were the Clash we'd actually have to play well.

If we hadn't gone to the States we might have just carried on going. We probably would have weathered the storm of punk and come out the other side. In the same way that Bowie and Roxy Music were able to come back later on, having been despised or reviled during that period, we could also have done that, but we didn't. The ludicrous thing is that we were feeling that we were really old hat and there was talk in the band that we were really old, that there were all these young punk people – who were actually the same age as us or older! – Bob Geldof, the guys from the Clash. It was odd.

But we were young and had no experience of this. Deaf School was basically our first real band, and we had no real perspective.

For Clive, at least, the record was an educational process, and set him on the path of his ultimate career. 'It was only after doing the album with Mutt Lange that I felt I knew something about the studio. I was just hanging out in the control room all the time. And Mutt Lange definitely knew what he was doing. He'd praise me when I'd say, "We could be doing this, or that." So I was using that dream of making records and Mutt was very receptive. But he didn't understand the Clash and I used to keep playing him the first Clash album. The only track that was given that treatment, and we argued about it, was "What a Week". "Leave it, it sounds great, don't put everything in its right place!" "English Boys" could have been a bit of a rocker but it sounds like Status Quo now. So I learned a lot from him, though I didn't really like his production.'

Enrico Cadillac is perhaps the least fond of *English Boys/Working Girls*:

> I never felt involved enough in the third album. Emotionally I wasn't feeling it. I didn't like what Mutt Lange was doing. I didn't want to sound like the Boomtown Rats. It's put together well but I don't think it's got a heart. There's a few moments there, 'Morning After', maybe, 'Thunder and Lightning', the songwriting and the tunes are still there, but the production was led by the record company. Understandably, it's the third album and they were looking for a break-out. Mutt Lange was our last drink in the Last Chance Saloon. If he couldn't make it work then who could?
>
> Maybe nobody could. Maybe you just have to do what you want and let people come to it. But a major company can't operate that way.

I've never listened to that album in the years following except for the Bette Bright tracks, which all have tremendous vocal performances, showing that she really is one of the great English vocalists. And that's where she started to sound like it. I have to credit Mutt with seeing it, and he is good with female vocalists. Bette Bright's stuff aside, that album missed the sound, soul, charm and wit of Deaf School. By the end of that we had lost the magic, for me.

It's quite true that Bette Bright excels, taking up a lot of the vocal space vacated by Steve. 'I found it amazing working with him,' she says of Mutt. 'He was really good at getting a performance out of a vocal. He knew how to get a good vocal, whatever happened with the album. Although we did sound like we had lisps.'

It's apt therefore that Ms Bright gets the third album cover to herself. (There had been a vague plan to feature individual band members on each successive sleeve.) 'It was probably just to give Bette a go at a cover,' thinks Kevin Ward. 'And we managed to get that amazing dress made. I don't know what that bar across was. I didn't want anything elaborate, I was going kind of minimalist, as the previous album had done. Although it wasn't black and white, it was pretty stark in terms of colour: red, white and black is a very strong combination. We actually bought a big white box and photographed against it.' The red dress she wore can nowadays be seen in a glass display case at the Museum of Liverpool, in the 'Wondrous Place' gallery that celebrates the city's popular culture.

***

Deaf School's third album was released in February 1978, to faint acclaim. Even a devotee like Holly Johnson confessed some disappointment. 'It somehow changed their true essence with a new straightahead rock direction,' he says on the band's website, 'not the Deaf School I knew and loved – the Deaf School that was a unique inspirational touchstone for a whole generation of creative rebellion and musical ambition that revived Liverpool's music scene after the Big Bang of the 1960s.'

Another new producer, Will Birch, was invited to try out some more tracks with Deaf School. He'd already done a little work with the Yachts, and was also drummer in the Records, coincidentally managed by Frank Silver: 'I now see them, looking back,' says Will, 'as a bit of a Trojan Horse for Clive Langer, a great guy and later a very successful producer. I do remember that Clive was very interested in being in the control room. Not in a pushy way, but he was a producer in the making, after all the art school shenanigans. He was very helpful.'

The two-day session was not a success. 'A complete disaster,' says Will, candidly. 'I had zero experience other than this Yachts single and that was quite easy, I had a reliable engineer and the record produced itself. But with Deaf School, because there were so many of them they were quite hard to marshal. We did it in a studio [Matrix] near the British Museum, and decided rather foolishly to meet in the pub on the corner, I think it was a Saturday lunchtime. And by the time the eighth member of Deaf School had actually arrived... I'd had a few drinks. But they were great to work with.' (Birch's previous band, artfully nostalgic pub-rockers from Southend called the Kursaal Flyers, once noted that Enrico wore a moustache like their own singer Paul Shuttleworth. The air was heavy, for a time, with accusation and reproach.)

Frank Silver flew once more to America, to present Deaf School's latest album to Warners and discuss the next US tour. As it turned out, he needn't have bothered.

* * *

Meanwhile there were British dates lined up. Ken Testi came along as a benevolent observer and was impressed: 'It had become an even more interesting show. You still had those touchstone numbers from the first album, but also Average's architectural pieces to punctuate, and then these great rocky things to spice it up and it's bloody brilliant. To this day with Deaf School you have the problem of what to leave out.' At the same time, however, he sensed that Clive Langer was carrying the burden of being group leader and chief songwriter, yet harbouring doubts about Deaf School's relevance to the altered landscape of British pop.

'To all concerned the band was in free fall around the release of the third album,' claims Average.

> We were called in to John Fruin's office at Warners – Derek had moved on by then – and he told us that it was make or break and that we could not have the same level of tour support that we'd had previously. So the tour that we did supporting that third album was done on a shoestring. We kipped on people's floors, we literally humped the gear ourselves from van to stage. As a band we did everything we could to keep it going. I don't think any of us minded the

hardship but the lack of return for our efforts up to that point was demoralising.

I handed in my resignation around March '78. Tensions within the group made it quite unpleasant to be in one another's company. I never fell out with anyone in particular. The whole situation was a pain. Neither was it helped, from my point of view, by the fact that my song 'All Queued Up' had been pulled at the last minute as our single... I got a phone call from Rob Dickins soon after my resignation during which he appealed to my better nature and asked me to stick with it until the end of the tour, ending 1 April, which I reluctantly did. I was the first one to formally exit the band.

I had that desire to go off and be in a band with four lads and have hits. I felt at that point for Deaf School there wasn't any evidence of a way forward. I know that even Clive had thoughts of working outside of Deaf School as well.

More than thoughts, Clive already had songs, written for a new project he wanted to call Clive Langer & the Boxes. 'Average had said he was leaving, which made me sad and left me thinking, What's the point now?'

Sam Davis, speaking in 1994:

The tour was strange because we were playing the same venues we'd played a year before, getting the same kids, but they were all punks. Big orange Mohicans and all that, but it was the same people. And it was considered *de rigueur* if you were a punk to show your appreciation by spitting on the band, so we had eight weeks of being covered in gob.

The same people coming to see us but their whole persona had changed. By that time we had a very exciting live show and we could play a bit, which helped.

But there were tensions starting to happen within the band. At one gig in Blackburn Steve the bass player wouldn't look at Tim the drummer, 'What the fuck are you doing?' and Steve hit one of his cymbals with the neck of his bass and Tim kicked the drums over in the middle of the set. At the same gig, Bette Bright, someone was jumping up and feeling her legs and she got so fed up she picked this bottle up and heaved it into the audience, which knocked this bloke out. Not the right bloke. So our manager of course is in total panic – law suits – so he goes diving into the audience, grabs this bloke, takes him backstage, he came round and says, 'But I'm a fan, I *like* the band!'

This gig was in fact at Wigan Casino, observed by the writer/broadcaster Stuart Maconie and described in his book *Cider with Roadies*. Bette Bright, who never had romantic notions about the rock lifestyle, certainly remembers them travelling in reduced circumstances: 'We had no road crew, and I was on list duty, so we'd do the gig and I'd be in charge of doing the van stack, everything in the right order. That was really quite hard to do, rather than just sashay off to your suite at your hotel.' Sam Davis had memories even closer to home: 'When we played at Birmingham we stayed at my mother's house, kipped on the floor, got up to bacon butties in the morning.'

Deaf School's final gig came at the end of that British tour, at the Liverpool Empire on 1 April 1978.

Their previous Empire show had been just one year earlier, on 11 March 1977, when they were inspiring a new generation into being. And a year before that, on 6 August 1976, the Empire hosted a *2nd Honeymoon* launch. Thus, Liverpool's grandest venue – a Lime Street variety theatre with scant connection to either Hope Street or Mathew Street – came to represent three stages in Deaf School's narrative arc.

***

Nobody knew for sure that night that this was Deaf School's swansong. Max Ripple was simply overwhelmed by the evident affection: 'Deaf School would not exist but for Liverpool. It's a co-created myth. I feel humbled by that. I would think, Why are they treating me so nice? I'm not even a Northerner, and yet there's a respect which I don't feel I deserve. At the last gig we did, at the Empire, somebody mentioned the Beatles and there was just this kind of incredible sigh, right through the whole place. It's like we were given some of that expectation.'

Average remembers it as the zenith of his Deaf School career: 'What was fantastic was, towards the end of the set, Bette Bright sings "Final Act", and that's my song. I move from the bass, which Clive can play, on to the keyboards, very simple chords. And just to stand at the back of the stage, look out at the Empire and to see two or three thousand people singing my lyrics back to the stage, is great. You can't beat that.

In fact I walked out of the Empire and went home and was quite relieved. It was a very stressful time, because when the success doesn't come, you need to have that commercial success to pay for the next phase. And when it doesn't happen, such a big band with a massive wage bill, the strain is quite significant. John [Max] had a family to pay for, Sam had a family as well, wife and kids. So they drew larger wages than everyone else, which was never a problem, but it was a real strain on them because their wages were minimal. When you're single you could live on fresh air, almost, but they had responsibilities. I remember Sam at that point having boils in his armpits, he'd walk around with pads under his arms. The poor guy, unbelievable, it was quite a problem.

Average had resigned in advance, but the others had not. The after-show party, at Steve and Anne's flat in Catharine Street, was simply a celebration and not a wake. There was even talk of another US tour. But Clive was rapidly losing heart.

For a while there were dark thoughts of slimming down the line-up. Average remembers it being discussed at a meeting in Catharine Street, with him and just three others. But it was not pursued. Bette has a glum memory of Frank Silver raising the idea on another occasion: 'We should scale the band down, there should be two singers and it should be Steve with either me or Eric Shark, that one of us should go. I don't know when it was, I have a vision of it being some place like Scarborough, somewhere with Bri-Nylon bed-sheets. Frightful.' Sam Davis recalled yet another scene: 'Our manager came up, he booked himself into the Adelphi and we were all called in to have an assessment. And it was like, "You've been a loyal member of the band, you're a good performer," and I'm

thinking, Why are you saying this? It was all pretty tense.'
But any such scheme was ultimately shelved. 'It was too
brutal for me,' says Clive. 'I loved everyone so much in
the band.'

This unhappiness within the ranks was mirrored by the
cold economic logic of the record company. With Derek
gone, Rob Dickins was nearly the only Deaf School fan
left in Warners' London office:

> There was still a belief that we could break through.
> In my whole career I've always thought you have
> to believe in what you do. Years later I remember
> meeting Madonna. I'd taken over the record company
> when her first single had stiffed ['Everybody', in
> 1982]. I remember having dinner with Madonna
> and getting that 'I'm gonna be the biggest artist in
> the world' from a girl whose first single had done
> nothing, and she was telling me she'd be the biggest
> act in the world. I've always used that example: if the
> artist does not believe that, and the next stage is the
> record company management, if they don't believe
> that, then it's probably not going to happen.
>
> So it continued. Derek spent the money, so they
> went on touring. It was a lot of people to put on the
> road but it pretty much always sold out. And we
> were coming from a period of the record industry
> where that was how you broke. You toured and you
> sold records and you built up a following and you
> waited for the break to happen. So we felt we had
> all the positives, and we were waiting for the break,
> and the break never came. And it wouldn't happen
> these days, they probably wouldn't have made
> album 2. They made three albums, so they had a

good shot. But it wasn't going to happen. It's always heartbreaking.

'The record sales weren't doing anything,' Sam reflected, 'and obviously Warners, by this time, had paid for us to go to the States, paid for three albums, a lot of money had gone through, I think it was about a quarter of a million by this time, and Derek Taylor had been shipped off to the States. John Fruin didn't like the third album, he wouldn't put any money into promoting it.'

The *coup de grace*, however, came with the question of Deaf School's next American tour. Under the financial circumstances, Fruin would naturally feel reluctance. What he did not expect, perhaps, was that Clive Langer was even more reluctant than he was: 'I went in and saw John Fruin personally, and said, Look, we *will* go to America, but I'd rather split up, so I'll leave it with you. We'll do our best there, we'll do everything you want us to do. But really, this is how I feel.

> If we'd done the second big American tour, maybe we could have built. And maybe I would have loved it, and that might have changed the whole direction of Deaf School. But it was like carrying a dead fucking weight. In my mind, I think the other members of the band didn't get what was happening, quick enough. I felt I couldn't express myself through Deaf School. The band seemed to be clinging on to what we were when we started and I just wanted to embrace punk and go beyond. I just felt, I want to move, and I'm not gonna move with you lot, cos you're all happy where you are.

And then about three weeks later Warners said,

'We'll drop you.' Financially we were costing them a fortune, we were using up all the Fleetwood Mac money that had come in.

In Average's recollection, 'I don't remember there being any real serious talk about a second tour of the US. Derek Taylor had long gone and I remember going into the Warners office and John Fruin saying, "Look, this is the reality of the situation." I do remember knowing that our days were numbered following that meeting. There was no more money. The writing had been on the wall for months. By the end of the UK tour our album sales were relatively poor, so I can't imagine Warners agreeing to bankroll another US tour at that stage. I don't remember it being anything more than just wishful thinking.'

Steve Allen, like Steve 'Average' Lindsey, has spent many years at the sharp end of the music industry since then, and takes a similarly understanding view of Warners' position:

I remember being in Catharine Street and getting a phone call from Clive saying the American tour's off. Frank had just heard that Warners were not going to put the money in to support the third album. Our whole plan was to go back to America with the third album, that was pencilled in. And Clive said, 'I think that's it.' Everyone had had time to digest the album and decide if this was going to make the difference that we need. Mutt Lange was supposed to bring us hits but maybe they didn't hear them. Our sense of direction wasn't intact. We'd lost our way on the second album, and punk was a tsunami that engulfed everybody. Warners would have needed a very good reason to go ahead with that tour, you can imagine how expensive it would have been. There had to be a hit on there that they felt was irresistible.

It's possible that someone suggested the band relocate to America and tour for a whole year or more – a tough but plausible strategy. Sam Davis did recollect the idea being floated: 'I said I would go. I would have quite enjoyed to live over there for a year, and Derek Taylor was there and he would have been another ally and done a lot of work for us. Certainly John Fruin wasn't prepared to put in any more money from England, but we knew we could have got money in the States.

'At the end of the day I think Clive vetoed it. He said No, he felt that it was a British band and it should be here and compete in the British market. I can't say it was a democratic decision, because it was all done privately, it was all secret ballot stuff. It got knocked back, and we just split up, and that was the end. It was either you do that or you split up.'

***

Today, Frank Silver sees their split as unavoidable: 'The first album sold around 15 to 20,000 pieces. It was always around that figure. It never took off above that. It was a cult thing. In America Warners managed to get the double album to about 76 for a week, but I think a lot of that was by manipulation of radio plays.

The group never sold significant numbers of records. And I would say there was a tailing off, even though the live offering grew from strength to strength. The singles never got the airplay that we hoped for, and the usual route was to get a single away and your album sales would follow. But the belief was this group were so strong live, that would power interest in them, and it was album sales that Warners expected, they didn't see them as a singles group but as an albums group of some quality and depth.

After three albums and plenty of touring, belief in the project was wearing thin. It was certainly getting harder for me to get more money out of Warners. I think there was an option coming up, and rather than have the ignominy of not having the option taken up, it just fizzled out. Creatively it had come to the end of the road. Derek was embroiled with other things in America and in the UK company the men in suits were making themselves felt.

The accountants took over and there was a much more professional attitude to things. With Warners and Derek it had been, 'We believe in your art and we will support it.' It was more artistic patronage than a commercial arrangement. It would be unthinkable today and it was becoming unthinkable in 1978.

The rest of the band received the news calmly. As Ian Ritchie puts it: 'When the album didn't do well and the breaking-up of the band was mooted, I think everybody just went, Yeah OK, that's fine. Time to do something else...' 'It was just kind of over,' considers Anne. 'Clive had moved on. It just felt like the time was right, and that was it. It wasn't like, "Oh my God! What's happened?" In fact I can't even remember it. It wasn't traumatic. It was a relief in a way.'

But two close friends of Deaf School were certainly caught unawares. Doreen Allen, Roger Eagle's assistant at Eric's, was being lined up to run a fan club for the band. And Norman Killon, DJ at Eric's, even planned his summer holiday around the US tour that never happened: 'I went over in advance, and the buggers broke up and didn't come over. I was over there waiting for them to arrive. I kept ringing Frank Silver and he'd say "I can't quite give you a date yet."' ('He was walking around New York with the T-shirt on,' says Steve. 'I felt bad about that for years.')

News of Deaf School's split appeared in the papers in the last weeks of April. A certain spin seems to have been agreed, blaming the band's demise on Warners' decision to pull the plug on a US tour. 'There was just no point in continuing as a group if there wasn't the money to promote our new album in America where the mass market is,' said Enrico to one music paper. There was unspecific talk of new bands emerging from the wreckage, but Eric Shark for one was not optimistic: 'The first thing I'll probably have to do is go and sign on the dole. That's sad.' A *Liverpool Echo* story ('Sound of Rock Fades for Deaf School') was equally downbeat, with Frank Silver telling of a fateful phone call from America, breaking news the contract was over.

But significantly, talking to *Record Mirror*, Clive has a more optimistic story: 'It wasn't commercially viable any more, after all there were eight of us in the band. We just weren't moving forward any more. The split was a good and positive one. I reckon there will be five new bands popping up after the split. We would like to thank all our fans especially those up north.'

***

Perhaps the last word should go to Derek Taylor, who could only view the final act from 5000 miles away. 'I had one or two failures,' he told me ten years later, in 1988.

I had Deaf School. I worked very enthusiastically for Deaf School, because I thought they were fabulous, and I used to bore the pants off people about them. I never saw the charts as being the real measurement of value. Real value doesn't necessarily end up in the singles charts.

You have to have faith in your own judgement. Long after it was all over, one of them, Sam, told me, 'We were always too big, there was too many of us, we were all over the place.' I said, Well, there was always that risk, you were too expensive to transport, every fare counted. And Warners spent a lot of money. But that didn't mean they weren't worth pushing, because they had real merit.

But I won't forget Deaf School. They were a great group, we knew that, you knew that, Liverpool knew that. So I'd be going 'Deaf School! Deaf School! Listen to Deaf School!' Like the Byrds, these are people who will never be forgotten. They may not become rich and they may not become famous. But remember, you heard it here first!

NINE

The Stopped Clock

Solo Lives – The Leaving of Liverpool
– That Next Phone Call

BETWEEN 1978 AND 1988 Deaf School had a ten-year half-life, as if cryogenically frozen. Its scattered members made new lives for themselves, with impressive success. Financially, if not emotionally, none of them needed Deaf School any more. Yet the dream never quite died. From carefree art school chancers they had become the Next Big Thing of a multinational corporation, until an abrupt divorce brought the whole adventure to an end. A sense of unfinished business has always lingered in these people.

Clive Langer moved back to London in 1978, feeling he had no further role in Liverpool if Deaf School weren't around. He shared a flat in Camden Town with Mel Haberfield, a co-founder of the Swanky Modes fashion shop downstairs, and they eventually married. Anne Martin, a fan of Swanky Modes designs, took another room in the same flat. In time, they were joined by a new resident, Suggs from Madness, who would duly marry Anne. A London network was replacing Liverpool.

Clive's priority, that year, was to get himself a band. He auditioned for Chrissie Hynde's new group the Pretenders, but the job would ultimately go to the gifted young player James Honeyman-Scott. (One might say this was a fortunate escape for Clive, as the Pretenders did seem cursed: in 1982 Honeyman-Scott died of a cocaine-related heart failure, while the bassist Pete Farndon, fired just two days before, died the next year of a heroin-related drowning. Ironically he was in the process of forming a group with Steve/Enrico.) This left Clive free to pursue his own dream of starting a band called Clive Langer & the Boxes. This was an ambition fulfilled, but also an effort to exorcise his previous band. 'Deaf School were who they were,' he says now, 'and I wanted to morph into something different. I was really excited by that.' He was rapidly signed to a new label, backed by Warners, called Radar. And the first EP set out his stall: '*I Want the Whole World*. And I wanted it now. It's going back to the Doors, it's aggressive. My hero Charlie Watts is in there, it's trying to be amusing in a Dury-ish, Robert Wyatt-ish vein.' Helping him out were Average on bass, the Liverpool drummer Budgie and on keyboards Ben Barson, of the North London Barson clan.

Also on Radar were his old Liverpool comrades the Yachts. The label's big star, however, was another graduate of the Merseyside music scene, Elvis Costello. Clive: 'The point of splitting Deaf School up was that I moved away. I wanted to be hanging out with the big boys. Luckily Elvis Costello was a fan of my first EP and that got me in with Jake [Riviera, Costello's manager]. So I left Frank Silver to go with Jake Riviera.'

Riviera signed both Clive and Costello to the new label he had founded, F-Beat. In 1979 Elvis asked to support Clive's band and the Yachts at a gig on the Mersey ferryboat *Royal Iris*. (Both acts could be forgiven if they felt a little upstaged by Elvis Costello & the Attractions storming through a set of numbers far better-known than their own material.) It was another step in the budding relationship between Langer and Costello: the latter had once approached the former at a Deaf School gig in Eric's to ask about his vintage suit. Soon they would each produce the 2-Tone label's earliest records, by Madness and the Specials respectively.

The Boxes now supported Elvis on tour, and he produced a few tracks on Clive's 1980 album *Splash*. Their connection would be picked up again a few years later. But Clive sensed that his solo venture was not shaping up: 'I lost my way a bit with the Boxes. Also I'd started recording other people and that seemed easier, and I didn't really enjoy being a frontman. I think *Splash* was the escape from Deaf School. I needed to do that. I could have then started a smaller Deaf School again. But Steve [Allen] and Ian [Broudie] had already started the Original Mirrors.' The Records' Will Birch remembers doing some writing with Clive at the Swanky Modes flat: 'He was understated, but it was a stealth mission. I got the impression he was biding his time, working with as many people as he could, networking a bit, gleaning a bit here and there from all these famous producers – and look what came out of all that.'

Clive's Madness connection, as already noted, had begun way before Deaf School and Liverpool art college. The band's Mike Barson, and his older brother Ben, went to Hampstead Comprehensive, but they lived near Clive's school William Ellis. 'I became friendly with Ben through my Hampstead friends,' says Clive.

Kids who had long hair around 1967, we interconnected the two schools. We were the hippy dreamers, experimenting with life. Ben Barson was a very close friend of mine. He was an incredible musician, much better than Mike technically, but his little brother was there listening, and banging away. They came to see Deaf School at the Roundhouse or the Nashville a couple of times; I'd see these kids and I'd wave to Mike while I was playing.

They were the coolest-looking kids around, amazing in the semi-skinhead North London thing that was après-hippy, a response to Kilburn & the High Roads. The Barsons were intelligent kids. Their mother was a painter and teacher; and Lee's family [Lee Thompson, eventual sax player of Madness], lived next door, so they were all mixed up.

But they had this band and asked, did I want to have a listen? I went to one of their rehearsals in this basement in the Finchley Road, and Mike sang 'My Girl'. Fucking hell! We all loved Robert Wyatt, that's where it came from, it's Soft Machine. Well, it's Robert anyway, and he was my great love.

It was 200 quid to go into Pathway Studios for two days of demos, which I didn't have. I'd left Deaf School and I had nothing. So I got Rob Dickins to pay for it, and he would own the masters. I said,

'Rob, trust me, 200 quid, we'll do these demos for you, this band The North London Invaders – or Morris & the Minors or whatever they were calling themselves at that point – they're brilliant.'

Rob Dickins takes up the story: 'He saw Madness and said, "I've found the band that I want to produce. Can you lend me some money?" So I did. There's a staccato thing that Clive had, which in Deaf School was not always commercial, but it worked with Madness because they were such a unit. They grew up listening to ska records, Dave & Ansell Collins, and when Clive came in and gave them these oddities, it gave them an identity above the other 2-Tone bands, that English identity that came from the Kinks and Ian Dury. Clive brought that and they embraced it. It was their unity and Clive's sensibility: had they been like Deaf School and all pulling in different directions, it wouldn't have worked.'

Clive: 'So Rob ended up owning "My Girl", "One Step Beyond" and "The Prince", one of the first singles released on 2-Tone, these demos suddenly became masters. That was my Barson connection into becoming a record producer, they were basically kids I knew who loved Deaf School, and I loved their family.' The tracks were evidence of Deaf School DNA in the Madness sound, such as the honky-tonk piano recalling 'Hi Jo Hi's channelling of Thunderclap Newman. Once you're conscious of the bands' relationship, it's easy to hear Deaf School in Madness. Their young singer, Suggs, was an avowed Deaf School fan: 'I remember things like that Thunderclap Newman solo, which became "Hi Jo Hi", and Clive talking about it when we did "My Girl" [Madness's 1979 hit single]. It's really off-key stuff coming out of a well-arranged pop song and going into something quite eccentric. He told us not to be scared of going eccentric sometimes. Deaf School were a big influence, for sure.'

From 2-Tone the band moved to Stiff, but Clive struck up an enduring production partnership with Alan Winstanley, house engineer at the small TW studio in Fulham that Rob Dickins liked to use. After the band's first album *One Step Beyond...*, Clive Langer & the Boxes supported Madness on the tour for their 1980 follow-up *Absolutely*, yielding more Langer/Winstanley hits such as 'Baggy Trousers', 'Embarrassment' and 'Return of the Los Palmas 7'. It seemed the chart success that always eluded Deaf School would now come Clive's way on a regular basis. He disbanded the Boxes and turned to full-time production. 'Post-Deaf School,' he says, 'there's a section of my life that gets glamorous and successful and completely different to the Deaf School story. Because where I ended up was doing production. I was suddenly propelled into the *successful* end of rock'n'roll. In the 1980s it was nice, it was like being a faceless star. I'd hang out with Madness – probably my best friend over the decade was Suggs – and I could enjoy being Clive Langer and not Cliff Hanger.'

Clive worked with Madness on all their subsequent hits, and noticed a certain parallel with something else. From the outset, Suggs & Co. were seen as rather lightweight in comparison with 2-Tone founding band the Specials. It reminded him of Deaf School's own travails in the time of punk. 'You're never taken seriously. Just because things are fun, it doesn't mean that down below there's not this content. Madness weren't political. They tried to be but they weren't. They were very different from Jerry Dammers.'

His studio career blossomed; he and Winstanley became Britain's most successful production team of the next two decades. Clive had already worked with the Eric's alumni The Teardrop Explodes; now signed to a major label, their manager Bill Drummond approached him to produce the band's next single 'Reward', and their second album *Wilder*. The former would prove the Teardrops' most lasting legacy, and Clive again credits Deaf School for his willingness to experiment with unusual instrumentation: the brash trumpet sound on 'Reward' was vital to the track's appeal.

Even greater glory came with Dexys Midnight Runners, the band fronted by Deaf School fan Kevin Rowland. With him, Langer and Winstanley co-produced the second album, *Too-Rye-Ay*, spawning the worldwide Number 1 'Come On Eileen'. The truth suddenly came to Clive: 'That's my career! I didn't plan to be a record producer, I didn't think I *was* a record producer until Dexys were Number 1 in America. I thought, Fucking hell, I have to give up this silly idea of being a rock star. I'm now a record producer.'

But he was still a songwriter. In 1982, while working on *Too-Rye-Ay*, Clive composed a uniquely haunting tune, inspired by hearing his old Canterbury idol Robert Wyatt sing the Billie Holiday classic 'Strange Fruit'. Recording a rough demo with Nick Lowe, he played the result to Elvis Costello (all three artists were clients of Jake Riviera). 'I couldn't write the lyrics,' Clive admits. 'I couldn't write anything that was worthy of the tune.' Fortunately, Costello could, and supplied a lyric based upon that year's war in the Falkland Islands. It was called 'Shipbuilding'.

Costello's Mersey roots embraced the shipyards on the

Birkenhead bank of the river; he conceived an ingenious story that married the district's chronic unemployment with the economic boost that comes with rearmament, set against the febrile atmosphere of a country gripped by wartime fervour. Over Clive's lurching, melancholic melody it made for a heart-rending combination. Robert Wyatt not only accepted the song but gave it one of the most affecting vocal performances in pop history. At the recording stage, he sang it to the composers from his wheelchair. Clive Langer drove away from the studio in his VW Golf and burst into tears.

Langer and Winstanley would work with Costello on his next two albums, *Punch the Clock* (containing its own powerful version of 'Shipbuilding', with the jazz trumpeter Chet Baker) and 1984's *Goodbye Cruel World*. If the latter was never a favourite of Costello's, he absolved its producers from the blame; they had helped him to his first US hit, 'Everyday I Write the Book'.

No graduate of any art school, let alone a graduate of Deaf School, could pass up the chance to work with David Bowie, and Clive's invitation came by way of his old schoolfriend Julien Temple. With Alan Winstanley he produced the soundtrack album for Temple's 1986 film *Absolute Beginners*, of which Bowie's title track remains the outstanding element. (At the same time it put Clive in the studio with other contributors including Ray Davies, Paul Weller and Sade.) At the same session they recorded Bowie and Mick Jagger's duet for Live Aid, 'Dancing in the Street'.

Bowie, he says, talked him out of another commission that came his way: 'We were doing *Absolute Beginners*, and I get a call to do Cliff Richard and The Young Ones.

[The cast of the TV sitcom, including Rik Mayall and Adrian Edmondson, planned a new version of Cliff's 'Living Doll' for Comic Relief.] And Bowie said "Don't do it." Cos we would have gone "Yeah, we'll do it, charity thing." Instead it was, "Sorry, we're working with David Bowie." So "Absolute Beginners" comes out and gets to Number 2 and it's stopped by The Young Ones! We could have been Number 1 and 2.'

Clive's other production credits are numerous, ranging from Alexei Sayle's 'Ullo John! Gotta New Motor?' and Marilyn's 'Calling Your Name', to They Might Be Giants' 'Birdhouse in Your Soul' and Morrissey's 'Kill Uncle'. So his solo career has been spectacular. Yet Clive Langer, more than anyone else in Deaf School, felt the band's absence. They say it's the same with an amputated leg.

***

Steve Allen, the former Enrico Cadillac Jnr, moved to London after Deaf School, just as Clive had done. He formed a new band, Original Mirrors, with Big In Japan's young guitarist Ian Broudie, who would in time become the Lightning Seeds. Rob Dickins, again, played a part: 'By now Steve and Ian Broudie were writing songs and I published both of them, so I helped them get a deal with Phonogram. But Phonogram never really understood them, they didn't have a sympatico record label.'

The band made two albums, *Original Mirrors* (1980) and *Heart Twango & Raw Beat* (1981) but their records never captured the power of Steve Allen's stage presence. His own view: 'Such a hot band, and ahead... The disco basslines and dancey grooves are what came later with

Duran Duran – who always came to see us at Barbarella's – and a bit of "Blue Monday" going on. I remember doing six encores on our first trip back to a rammed Eric's, post-Deaf School, various Teardrops, Bunnymen, Wah, Icicle Works, Lotus Eaters, Big In Japaners, Colin Vearncombe [of Black] in the audience, a barnstorming gig. Bette B and Clanger came up, Clive came backstage with a shocked look on his face and said "Fuck me! What a band."'

Steve Allen was left wondering what to do next: 'I was in two failed bands when I was trying to find a new way after Original Mirrors. I started a band with Topper Headon [from the Clash], Pete Farndon [Pretenders] and Henri Padovani [the Police], and another band with Glen Matlock [Sex Pistols]. Pete Farndon died in the bath while we were waiting for him to turn up at a rehearsal. After that I got out for a while, because it upset me a lot. I'd never been involved with heroin in bands. I was in bloody Deaf School, for God's sake. There were no drug addicts in Deaf School. We never even got groupies! So to be in a band with people like Topper, and then Pete Farndon dies in the bloody bath…

'I left England and went to live in Paris. I needed a real cleansing of everything and didn't want to be in a band. I went solo and had some hits, didn't care what it was, really. It was quite cathartic.' Through the 1980s Steve Allen scored some European disco-pop successes, released under his real name (ironically, for a man who once traded with a cod-Latin one), and in 1986 tried a brief liaison with Elvis Costello's keyboard player Steve Nieve, called The Perils of Plastic. Eventually, with his new partner Vanessa (and with their young son,

Alexandre, in tow), he called time on the continental experiment:

> I had one very bad year in Paris. That's when I came back to England, I just couldn't get on with the ways of the French music industry. I guess I knew too much and I just had too much to forget to operate on the required level, which was very poor at that time to my ears. I loved and still love Paris, but things never stopped looking up for me when I came back to England. Within a year I signed Vanessa's band, Espiritu, to Heavenly Records and they had four chart hits.

He was quickly hired by Rob Dickins to do A&R at Warners. 'I hired him because he liked things I hated. He liked Euro-pop. When you run a small label, it's about you. But Warners or CBS or Phonogram, it's not about you any more. You have to piece together the jigsaw of a major record company. Steve would talk about this French record, this German record, so I said, Come and work for me and just do that. And he had hit after hit after hit. Singles. It's now become mainstream but at the time he was on the cutting edge of Euro-pop coming into this country. Steve brought in that area that I didn't care for, and gave us success.'

Indeed, in parallel with Clive's stellar progress as a producer, Steve became one of Britain's top A&R men. 'When I started at Warners in '93,' he says, 'I pretty quickly realised that I didn't want to be part of the standard A&R thing, all going to the same gigs. I didn't really want to get involved with signing bands. So I went for my own label. I picked up this label that was dormant, Eternal Records.

And I basically signed all those cheesy pop dance records. It was a good way for me not to have to field calls from everyone I knew in the industry who had a band. And I suddenly started signing hit after hit after hit.'

Through Eternal (a label which, by coincidence, was originally created as a vehicle for Liverpool's Pete Wylie and Wah!) and other parts of Warners, Steve was key to numerous success stories, including Everything But The Girl, Danni Minogue, Gina G, Corona, Eiffel 65, Dario G, Black Legend and Holly Valance. ('All good healthy cheesy pop,' as he likes to put it.) 'I'm quite pleased, when I look back, that I found Clive Langer, that I found Ian Broudie, and I wasn't even an A&R guy at the time. And later I found Brian Higgins, who's done all the Girls Aloud stuff [as producer and co-writer] with Xenomania. I signed him. And I signed Brian Rawling, the Metrophonic guy, who produced Cher's "Believe", and Enrique Iglesias and all this pop stuff.'

Today, Steve Allen runs his own company, Rushmore Recordings, where he manages Vanessa & the O's: 'We're the baby boomers,' he says, 'we're the ones who got it all, and it's not fair on those who came later. Born in the '50s, it was a pretty good time. When your first records are the Beatles or the Stones, it's not bad. And then you've still got Bowie and Roxy to come.'

***

Anne Martin moved down to London with Steve in 1979. 'When I got the advance on my publishing for the Mirrors,' he says, 'me and Anne went off on holiday. But the magic had sort of gone and then she met Suggs, although we stayed friends. She was living in Swanky Modes by then.' She had already formed her own band, Bette Bright & the Illuminations, backed for live shows by Clive, Glen Matlock, Henry Priestman and Rusty Egan. This was an illustrious line-up. Priestman, of the Yachts, would soon make many hits with the Christians. With Matlock and Midge Ure, Egan had been in the promising but short-lived Rich Kids, becoming a scene-making DJ and producer in the new romantic and acid house eras.

Signed to Radar, Bette's 1978 single was 'My Boyfriend's Back', followed by 'Captain of Your Ship', entertaining takes on 1960s soul-pop. 'But it was really difficult,' she told me in an *NME* interview in 1981, 'because Radar were limited with finances – I ended up paying for most of that tour myself. I think they spent most of their budget on Nick [Lowe] and Elvis.' Courtesy of Rob Dickins, she moved to Warners' Korova label: 'Such a great band,' he says. 'And because they weren't doing original material, they could actually enjoy themselves. We got a little smell of success with that but not enough.' Her singles included Prince's 'When You Were Mine' and the eventual album was *Rhythm Breaks the Ice*, produced by Langer and Winstanley. She even played that plastic sax sometimes. 'I suppose I'd really like to be the Lulu of the '80s.' she told me. But that was not to be.

Instead, apart from marrying her Swanky Modes flat-mate (and Langer production client) Suggs McPherson of Madness, she played a guest role in another sprawling art rock outfit, Holland's Gruppo Sportivo. She appeared fleetingly in *The Great Rock'n'Roll Swindle*, a film of the Sex Pistols' story as re-imagined by Malcolm McLaren, written and directed by Clive's friend Julien Temple.

And, in due course, Mr and Mrs McPherson had two daughters, Scarlett and Viva. Deaf School reunions apart, she was never tempted back into a musical career: 'When my dad died it made me realise that life is temporary. Then when I had Scarlett, and Suggs was really busy with Madness, I just felt I wanted to be a mother, I wanted solidity in my life. And I felt I'd had enough of it all. I'd been doing it for a big chunk of my life. I wasn't hankering to be famous.'

More recently, Anne has been assailed by illness: 'I had breast cancer,' she says, with casual stoicism. 'And now my voice is really husky. I've found this at rehearsals, I can sing, but it goes really easily. I think that's to do with the chemotherapy. It just made it huskier. Which is all right. The trouble is, all those Deaf School songs are in keys that are ridiculous, they're so high. So... I was a bit ill and that was all quite dreary, quite frankly. But anyway, it's fine.'

***

Steve Lindsey, Mr Average, occupied his downtime after Deaf School with a quick stint in the local act who were in a way their elected successors, Big In Japan. 'As Deaf School went our separate ways,' he says, 'we were very aware of how potent the new generation behind us was. I certainly saw Eric's as the catalyst for all that. But what Deaf School added to Eric's was, "Jeezus! If *they* can do it, anyone can." We opened it up.' He played some 'guerrilla gigs' with BIJ members Ian Broudie and Budgie, plus Dave Hughes of Dalek I Love You, calling themselves the Secrets. He made a couple of singles, billed once as Mr Average and once as Steve Tempo.

'We did keep in touch,' he says of his fellow Deaf Schoolers. 'There was never animosity. We all had our publishing deal with Warner Brothers Music, who had a studio where we'd help each other out on demos. We'd dip in and show our faces, so there was a fair amount of interaction. I played bass when Clive did his solo EP with the Boxes. It was nice to be asked by him to provide bass because he liked what I did. But when I struck out on my own, I didn't get the assistance of any of the previous band members. I suppose I just wanted a complete change. It was a relief to put it behind us.'

His new band was called the Planets: still managed by Frank Silver they endured a galactic photo shoot in space suits on the roof of the London Planetarium. They signed to Rialto, a small label whose publishing was done by Rob Dickins. 'It was a totally different kettle of fish,' says Average. 'When I was a kid and growing up with the Beatles, I wanted to be in a four-piece band, all male, that could go out and shag and sell records. And as a songwriter I also loved singles, good tunes that ended up being anthems. So the Planets was set up to be that sort of thing, and we did make our mark in a modest way on the charts, and did *Top of the Pops*.'

It was a 1979 single, 'Lines', from the Planets' first album *Goon Hilly Down*, that secured the coveted *TOTP* appearance. This achievement has never been lost on the others in Deaf School: 'Average was the only one who ever did *Top of the Pops*,' remarks Clive, 'which we all wanted to do.' Another track, 'A Minute Ago', revisited the popular Deaf School number 'Darling'. A press release of the time notes the success other Deaf School alumni were having (Clive, Bette and Steve Allen) and adds, 'The half-million pounds that that Warner Brothers spent on the band should now make a profit for other companies. Bugs Bunny strikes again.'

In the Planets' case, and sadly for Rialto, this was far from certain. A disappointing second album, 1980's *Spot*, met with a quiet response. By 1982 the band was defunct. Three years later Lindsey/Average was working for the music publishers Chappell, who in 1987 became part of the omnipresent Warners. A year later he was general manager at the hip independent Go!Discs. He found himself assisting Liverpool's next cult legends, the La's, on their most celebrated song: 'I was working really hands-on with the La's, I did their live sound, I helped with their recordings. I played the bass on "There She Goes": there's two basses on there, I played the low bass. And that was the release that got to about 41 in the charts, didn't quite hit it.

'Then I worked with Beats International, Norman Cook [aka Fatboy Slim], again in an A&R role, a supportive pair of ears for him. I did the radio edit of "Dub Be Good to Me". I was delighted when Andy MacDonald [Go!Discs boss] called me into his office: "Steve! I've got something for you!" And it was a gold disc for "Dub Be Good to Me". Then I went downstairs to show everyone, and everyone else had got one.'

Though Average is self-effacing, others in Deaf School report that he was an outstanding figure behind the scenes at various companies. He became general manager at Island Music, handling the publishing for acts including the Beautiful South, U2, Pulp and Massive Attack. He branched into movie music supervision, *Mission Impossible* being one of his projects, and set up a publishing company with Robbie Williams' managers. In the early 2000s he moved to Dublin and married the writer Fiona Looney: 'I met my wife-to-be as a result of working with so many Irish acts and it was natural to spend time there. While I was at Island we signed the Cranberries, we had ongoing relationships with U2 and Gavin Friday.

'It was probably the end of the golden era of the music business that had arisen during the '60s and '70s when there was lots of money sloshing around.' In 2004 he set up his own publishing company, Elevate Music, representing composers across the spectrum. On its current roster is a band called Deaf School.

***

The Reverend Max Ripple now wears the alternate title Professor John Wood DipAD ADF (Manc) FRSA. 'Actually,' he confesses, 'I was quite surprised to get back into art academia.' Nevertheless, of all Deaf School's members, he had been the most settled in a previous vocation and moved swiftly back into teaching and art practice. Music and sonic experimentation remained close to his heart: teaching at Wolverhampton he became involved in a Portsmouth Sinfonia-type project. 'I was playing piano, there was no agenda and everyone played anything and we had about four hours of improvisation. Then when I moved to Goldsmiths [the prestigious South London college], I had a little group there in the '80s, all basically sculptors, and we called ourselves the Kreutzer Quintet. We had Grenville Davey who was a Turner prize winner and he played buckets of sand and stepladders, twatted them with a hammer and stuff like that.' His students at Goldsmiths would include Graham Coxon of Blur: 'So there is a thread,' says Max, 'that runs through these art schools in Britain. I've worked with Gustav Metzger, who's in his 80s, a celebrated artist, who taught Pete Townshend at Ealing. And one of his big ideas was auto-destructive art, and an obvious influence on the Who smashing up the equipment.'

Now married to the artist Alma Tischler Wood, he formally retired from Goldsmiths in 2010, having also taught Fine Art to various YBAs, the Young British Artists movement that was centred on the college. His main area is metadesign, defined as 'designing in a very practical manner using environmentalist and ecological principles to achieve a sea-change in society's lifestyle'. He's also worked extensively in the Far East: 'Technically, I've retired, but at the same time I've got this Emeritus Professor thing, and they've asked me to do some more teaching there. If we play in Tokyo again, I would maybe stay around and go to Korea and Taiwan. I'm still struggling with deadlines, writing papers, doing PhD exams.'

* * *

For his part, when Deaf School split Ian Ritchie faced an uncertain future with acceptance:

> I didn't think about it. I wasn't a career musician who'd decided when I was young that this was what I was going to be. I was just on some weird path that I didn't really understand. I definitely knew that Deaf School had run its course. But they were my first band and this hadn't happened to me previously. At that time *Melody Maker* had ads at the back

for musicians, and some of them were actual jobs: 'Circus needs saxophone player' or whatever.

So I auditioned in Wales for a dance band in the Locarno Ballroom or something, and I didn't – luckily – get in. And one of the other ads was from a singer-songwriter in London who had a publishing deal. So, fairly shortly after breaking up, I relocated to London. I remember sleeping on Frank Silver's floor for a few nights.

The singer-songwriter's band turned out to be a dud. Ian was already finding that nothing quite matched the fun of Deaf School. For a while he turned to busking. 'I'd go down to South Kensington tube station with a flute or a soprano saxophone, and the Americans going to the V&A Museum down that tunnel thought this was culture. Particularly if I had some music up, which I was learning to read at that time. So I did OK out of that. And being in that area, in the evenings there used to be lots of restaurants that had live acts, so I would sit in and they would feed me.'

Over time he became a busy sax player, arranger, composer and producer. Sessions ranged from the briefly hip new wavers Jane Aire & the Belvederes to Wham!'s 'Club Tropicana'; he formed a new band Miro Miroe, who charted with the single 'Nights of Arabia'. He wrote and performed numerous TV themes and adverts, including the *Lonely Planet* series, and was an early adopter of 1980s computer technology and its musical applications, setting himself up for further success as a producer with everyone from Liverpool's Pete Wylie and Wah! to New York's Laurie Anderson. Perhaps his greatest collaboration was with Pink Floyd's Roger Waters, producing the solo

Radio K.A.O.S. album and subsequently playing with him live across the globe. He currently lives in North London with his wife and co-performer Holly Penfield.

***

After Deaf School, their manager Frank Silver spent several more years in artist management, including the Slits, Comsat Angels and the Jam's producer Peter Wilson. He eventually moved into the property business:

> My role with Deaf School, apart from that negotiation process, was managing the day-to-day activities of the group, and there were eight or ten of them, all of whom were intelligent, articulate, opinionated, with attitudes to everything: artwork, touring, road crew. It became for me an absolute blur. I worked like a dog for three years. The world was still Dickensian in many ways. There were micro-negotiations every day: can we get the van cheaper, can we get the cheapest hotel that's not too ghastly, etc.
>
> I wouldn't say managing Deaf School was pleasurable. It was intense. But it was fascinating. I look back on it now and think, what an extraordinary period of my life. I realise I'm an incidental player in the group's story: they were full of artistry, energy and invention. There were some volatile heads in the group, it wasn't always calm. There were even times I had to talk to Clive and Steve to cool out their relationship.
>
> Artists in all their forms are hard work. They're demanding, mercurial, very emotional. Having to mediate that was very wearing. So I thought to

myself, Bricks and mortar don't answer back. So that's what I parked my money in.

But I wouldn't have any of my wealth and security today without Deaf School starting me off. So I feel grateful to them for allowing me to be their manager. It altered my life incredibly. Who knows what I might be doing otherwise? I might still be bouncing people at the door of the Roundhouse.

* * *

Sam Davis, like Ian and Average, completed his course; he came away from art school with a 2:1 BA (Hons) as well as some practical teaching experience. After the split he did go on the dole at first, as he'd told the press. He worked with Kevin Ward, the two men sharing a studio, and they had a few musical sessions with Steve Allen. 'We were the original Original Mirrors,' he said in 1994. 'Then Steve went off and got this band sorted and said "D'you mind if I use that name?" No, help yourself.

> I was married and I had two kids so there was pressure to earn money. I worked for Frank's management company and I'd do things like fly out to Berlin to meet that punk band the Slits. I had to take some guitars out, rehearse them for a few days and do a few gigs. That was before they'd signed up and I think Frank was trying to get them sorted but that was pretty wild. They took me on shoplifting sprees around Berlin. I'm sure I could have gone and worked for a record company or management company in London, but I ended up with a shop in Widnes.

I hated it, it was like prison to me. So I packed that in, went on the dole again, and somebody offered me a teaching job. So I went back into teaching and found, possibly because of all the things I'd done, that I could be quite successful at that and got promoted fairly quickly and was earning quite a lot of money again. And then you're in the wealth trap because you're earning a few bob. And then I got in touch with Geoff again.

Geoff Davies, from the Probe shop, now had his Probe Plus label and Sam joined him in developing its acts. 'We managed Half Man Half Biscuit together,' says Geoff, 'and produced quite a lot of Probe Plus records under the name the Bald Brothers. Sometimes it just says "produced by" and you see a half a circle with things sticking out of it, as if to say not much hair. That was Steve Hardstaff's invention, the Bald Brothers logo.' But the pressure of full-time teaching persuaded Sam, in the end, to exit the music business for the foreseeable future. Which was all very well, except that members of Deaf School are never more than one phone call away from going back.

And sooner or later, there *would* be a phone call.

TEN

That Thread of Affinity

The Second Coming – Suggs in the House –
Remembering Tim Whittaker and Sam Davis

IN 1988 A SHORT tour brought Deaf School back together,
ten years after their last show. Team spirit seemed
miraculously restored and their audience were no less
committed. Where 1978 had been a year of frustration
and resignation, 1988 revealed new creative energy. It
brought a dawning recognition that being in Deaf School
– rather as Derek Taylor had said of the Beatles – brought
life membership.

Ken Testi, the band's old mentor and tour manager, had
by now returned to his ancestral calling and was running
a pub in the Cheshire village of Eaton. But he was restless.
It was more than a decade since he'd left Eric's, and *la vie
en rock* was calling once more. 'I was on to my second

pub now, the Red Lion, and I hadn't had a breather. I had a four-acre site in a nice country village and I got the itch for another Deaf School show. I said to Clive it was time to do this and amazingly he said "Right. Brilliant!"' To make the reunion viable they would need more dates. A few small shows were set up in London, beginning at Camden's Dublin Castle on 14 June; two bigger shows were booked at Hardman House in Liverpool and finally a marquee in the field by Ken's pub, on 25 June.

Clive: 'The '88 thing's weird, because I was very busy. But obviously I had a few months free. It was the anniversary, ten years since we'd finished. I just thought, What a great idea. Let's do it. Why not? Everyone seemed to jump at it. Tim couldn't do it, because he'd been in a car accident and so we had to get a different drummer. But everyone else could apart from Ian, and wanted to.' Sam Davis, by now teaching art full time, recalled the obstacles:

> Clive just phoned me up, drunk: 'Get your guitar out, you're playing.' So I said OK. I was still working at the time so the rehearsals were a bit difficult, cos I'd go down to London and have to drive back through the night to go to work the next day. It was three or four gigs in London before we did the ones up here, which is a bit weird, warm-up gigs in London. But they were great cos they were just like parties. But again the same thing, I'd hire a car, drive down after work, do the gig, drive back, go to work and try and pretend nothing had happened, that I'd been at home in bed.

Steve Lindsey needed no persuading:

That feeling of belonging to a club, that thread of affinity, it never went away. So it wasn't a surprise when I got a call from Clive saying 'It's ten years since we split up. It's time to do another gig!' By that time I'd done the Planets, got into music publishing, so I was, Oh, OK, I'd better remember how to play the bass again. I'd made a conscious decision, when I got into the business side, to put all that behind me. I'd put that 'Don't you want to *make it*?' attitude to bed. Move on and join the real world. So there was a side of me going, Oh God... But everyone else wanted to do it and secretly I suppose I did too.

It was a joy to get involved. Clive had had a lot of success by that point, as a producer of Madness, etc. So that gave the whole experience some spice and impetus. I was still totally embroiled in the record business and the world of publishing. For me it was a nice few weeks' diversion.

Max Ripple, busy teaching art and quite detached from the music business, was less prepared: 'It crept up on us a bit. It hadn't occurred to me that it might happen. I was thinking, No, this is the worst direction I can go in.' Nevertheless, he agreed. But Ian Ritchie did not take part: 'I was in the middle of an album,' he explains, 'and I just couldn't go back for it. And actually I was in a completely other place by then; even if I'd been in London I'm not sure that it would have seemed like an attractive proposition at that time. I don't know.'

In the event saxes were played by Lee Thompson of Madness and the prolific session man Gary Barnacle. On drums, deputising for Tim Whittaker, was Martin Hughes from Clive Langer & the Boxes. There were guest appearances by Suggs (alias Mr Bette Bright), Henry Priestman and David Bowie's guitarist at that time, Reeves Gabrels. 'What was brilliant,' says Average, 'was that Nick Lowe supported us at the Hardman House gigs and the gig out in Chester as well. It was wonderful to see people just congregating, that the magnetism was still there. Gobsmacking. Again, one of the highpoints was Nick Lowe came on for the encore and played "What's So Funny Bout Peace Love & Understanding".'

Hardman House, a hotel in those days, stands across the road from O'Connor's, where Deaf School's public life had begun fourteen years previously. The show was a little less theatrical than before, and the sight of Enrico *sans* moustache took a little adjustment, but the atmosphere was just as magical as Average says. 'When we got to Liverpool it was amazing,' says Clive. 'It was ten years and there suddenly seemed a reason.' Bette Bright, by now more elegant than camp ('becoming a lady with a past,' as Derek Taylor had put it), recalls it as 'really strange. Years had gone by but it felt like yesterday.'

Sadly, Hardman House was to be Deaf School's last encounter with Derek Taylor. Promoting the shows, Geoff Davies of Probe spotted Derek at the door, paying to get in because nobody had put him on the guest list. 'I didn't even know he was going to be there,' says Enrico. 'That's when I first came back from Paris, where my son had just been born. I came over to do the gigs with Deaf School and brought Vanessa with me, a drop-dead gorgeous young French girl, and Derek was like "Wow! Who's this?" I said, This is my girlfriend Vanessa. Actually, she doesn't know anybody and doesn't speak much English, would you mind – And he went, "Being her chaperone? Absolutely *charmed*." He looked after her, though she didn't have a clue who he was until years after, watching the film of John and Yoko in their hotel room.'

'My sad thing,' says Clive, 'is that I didn't see him when he was dying, and I didn't see him much after Deaf School. He came in '88 and someone had forgotten to put his name on the door, probably me, but he got in and I saw him as we finished the gig. But I was just too wrapped up in the mayhem and getting a drink; I spoke to him but I just wish I'd given him more attention. Because he gave *us* a lot of attention, and he was so loved and appreciated.'

More happily, the Hardman House shows were captured by Clive for posterity: 'We had this recording truck outside for two days. Luckily I owned a studio and I didn't charge. There was never any money about. The album took about three weeks to mix, because we were patching things up and trying to make it acceptable.' Indeed, there are many (Sam Davis was one of them) who hold *2nd Coming* to be the best Deaf School record of all. There are some nice rarities: the unreleased 'Princess Princess', the Flamin' Groovies' 'Shake Some Action', the Planets' hit 'Lines' and a smoky lounge version of 'Blue Velvet' (which had recently been revived with a sinister twist in David Lynch's movie of that name). But above all are barnstorming versions of the core songs in Deaf School's live repertoire: 'What a Way to End it All', 'Taxi' and 'Capaldi's Café', capped with 'Final Act', in all its languid melodrama.

Despite the excitement of the tour – and the night in Ken Testi's field made for a memorable finale – the Deaf School gang were still embroiled in 'real' careers and in most cases had young families to raise. Apart from a

1989 benefit for the Hillsborough Appeal – Deaf School had a natural sympathy with the families of 96 Liverpool football fans killed on that atrocious day in April – the band slipped back into its slumbers. This hiatus would last sixteen years.

***

And one founding member would never rejoin them. Tim Whittaker died on 20 July 1996, aged 43.

Tim had not played any Deaf School reunion gigs, bowing out on the Liverpool Empire night in April 1978. Steve Lindsey, for one, reckons that was the last time he saw him. An 'injury' kept the drummer off their 1988 tour, but it's generally thought he couldn't face it. According to Sam Davis, 'Tim didn't play, because he felt he wouldn't be good enough after all this time. He felt he couldn't get it back together this fast.' As Enrico remembers, 'He said he had a problem with his arm or his shoulder. I remember that Clive was a bit cynical about it, and was gutted because he loved Tim.

> But my reaction was, Well, he always had that fear. Like Ringo with George Martin at those first recordings, he thought he was going to go soon. He felt he wasn't good enough to be in a proper band with a record deal. Even though we reassured him: 'You are part of us, mate, you are Deaf School.' He thought Mutt Lange or someone might think, 'I might bring someone in to cover some of these tracks.' That might have been mentioned but we said, 'No way, we're not arsed whether he speeds up or slows down.' That's the world we were going into,

where every drummer's got to be constant, like a clock. We didn't want a drummer like that.

Tim had already completed his art degree when Deaf School signed to Warners, and remained a painter for the rest of his life. 'His work was really well received,' says Sandra Harris. 'All the tutors rated him as an artist.' As Rob Dickins recalls: 'Tim Whittaker became a pretty good action painter. I always liked him because, as a Londoner, he was what I wanted a Northerner to be. He used to say he was from "Accrington DC".'

But Tim remained at the heart of the Liverpool music scene, playing on Bill Drummond and Dave Balfe's records for Lori & the Chameleons ('Tim was our guru,' wrote Bill; 'whatever Tim said sounded like it carried the wisdom of a sage') and with Jayne Casey's band Pink Military. He had a fantasy group that he called Truncheon Leader of Youth, a real band called Divine Thunderbolt, and formed the semi-mythical Sex Gods with Echo & the Bunnymen's drummer Pete de Freitas (who switched to guitar). 'I met Tim around the time that Deaf School first split up,' says the Liverpool DJ Bernie Connor. 'He was always in Eric's.

> He was older than me but we hit it off and spent huge periods of time taking acid together and sorting it out. All the time he was painting and painting, and in 1983 he moved into Aigburth Drive with the Bunnymen. They took to him as a very important person in their make-up. He bonded with Pete over drums and percussion and showed him a lot about the space in his rhythm. Everything they did they wanted Tim's nod of approval.

The Sex Gods thing was Tim's mad idea: 'What's your group called?' We're the Sex Gods of course!

Tim was my best friend, and one of the few people I hero-worshipped. In 1992 he turned up at ours for Christmas dinner, and he had nothing to give us, so he handed us a 29-page handwritten poem [*Liverpoem*, reprinted in the Appendix]. Which is incredible. He was a great drummer and his influence beyond Deaf School, Tim as the psychedelic guru, is fantastic.

He was very dry and droll in his Lancashire way. He had the strangest accent, proper 'Bah gum!' He'd say the most wonderfully strange things. He was a very private fella, in a way. We could live in the same house and sometimes go for months without saying hello. But I never thought that was him being aloof or rude. It's just the way he was, a great artist, a great painter. He had great ideas but he was not cut out for the art world.

He illuminated lots of people's lives. He had this thing about Al Jackson Jnr, the drummer out of the MGs. He went to see the Jimi Hendrix Experience in Manchester when he was about 14 and Mitch Mitchell the drummer came out of the dressing room and shook hands with him. He was bowled over. He had this old radiogram in the house in Harrowby Street off Princes Avenue, you know the ones where the arm just goes backwards and forwards? He just went to his Mum's for the weekend and left side 1 of *Axis: Bold as Love* playing. A fantastic cat. I miss him a great deal.

* * *

The band was in abeyance, but the members of Deaf School kept in touch over the years, with the London-based trio of Clive, Enrico and Bette especially close friends. 'I'd go to Clive's and late at night we'd have a few drinks,' remembers Steve Allen:

> He'd reach for a Deaf School album and I'd say, If you go any closer to that album I'm going! And he'd go, 'Just a couple of tracks.' Which album? *Don't Stop the World*? No, *2nd Honeymoon*. He goes, 'OK!' Next thing, three hours later, we've listened to everything.
>
> And Anne's sitting there going, 'That's really good, that. I told you, that was *always* really good.' And I just hadn't listened to it for a long time, I'd put it all away. I think it was only when we did the Magnet, when Kevin Rowland and Suggs came on, for Steve Lindsey's birthday, that was the first time I agreed, because he had tried to get me to do things before, and I'd go, No, I'm in another life now, I can't connect to that. It was only when we did the Magnet that I actually felt that connection and I felt the crowd again. I felt the love, the unrequited love of Deaf School fans. Which is pretty strong. And it wasn't a bad gig. Very rough, we hadn't even worked it out properly but that was it.

The Magnet was a turning point in Deaf School's story. For his 50th birthday party, in 2005, Steve Lindsey dreamed up a private gig in Liverpool. The Magnet is a basement club in Hardman Street, nearly opposite the former O'Connor's (which by now housed a costume-hire business) and yards away from Hardman House. Historic Deaf School links aside, the Magnet was in former times the Sink Club, an important venue for beat bands, rhythm & blues fans and, of course, the site of Freddie Mercury's first appearance with Taylor and May, at the Ibex gig in 1969. It was a night of high emotions.

For Ian Ritchie, it was his first return to the fold since Deaf School Mark I. Like the others, he was reaching a point in his life where there was more space to play with:

> It was great. When Clive and I were doing lots of production, you're in the studio all the time, you don't have the energy to do much outside of that. Whereas by the time Steve's birthday came up, I'd moved into composing for TV, doing adverts and stuff. I'd started playing jazz gigs again. I remembered that the reason I started in music in the first place was because I love to play. My fondest memories of Deaf School are of being on stage with them. They're the band I remember having the most fun playing with. So when Clive contacted me I was totally up for it. It was only supposed to be a few songs but expanded to almost a set. I'm not sure we even expected everybody to even turn up, but the whole band did.

In what became a counter-intuitive habit, they began with 'What a Way to End it All', and by the set's end had thrilled the small room's jam-packed audience with a classic Deaf School show, joined on 'Thunder and Lightning' by Suggs and by Dexys' Kevin Rowland, who then duetted with Bette on the old Illuminations' favourite 'Hold On I'm Coming'. Graham Fellows, the creator of both Jilted John and John Shuttleworth, was on stage at one point. And Mike McCartney, from Scaffold, was down at the front along with nearly everyone from Deaf School's Liverpool circle.

For Bette the show had an even more intimate resonance. Her daughters, Scarlett and Viva, had come along for the 1988 shows but slept soundly throughout. 'So they had never seen me singing until we played at Average's birthday. Johnny [Clive's son] and my two daughters were crying because they'd never heard Deaf School. It was sweet that they were all in tears: "My God, was it that dreadful?" But no, they were all just emotional. So once we got *that* sorted out...'

Sam Davis, back in his Eric Shark guise, was clearly enjoying himself, but was just as clearly unwell. His widow Joan:

> He'd always had trouble with his lungs. He'd had whooping cough when he was a kid, and was still struggling with that. But he was still singing. Even a consultant said 'Carry on singing, it's great for your chest.' He developed this thing called bronchi-ectasis, where your lungs fill up with crap, but he still performed with the band even with his oxygen on. It kind of suited the persona! I mean, if you're going to go out, go that way.
>
> He came out of hospital that day, he'd just started to be really ill. He was in Broadgreen and he told the consultant, 'I have *got* to come out because it's my friend's 50th birthday.' The consultant probably thought it was just a party and didn't realise he'd be singing. So he came and he was a bit weak but his voice came back after that. But he loved it and it

was great for all of them to slip back into that again. They were freed up from the pressure of having to make it. They could just enjoy it.

Kevin Rowland had good reason to share a stage with these people. Years before Clive Langer produced Dexys' biggest record, Rowland was in the Deaf School audience at Barbarella's Club in Birmingham. In a 2012 interview with *NME.com*, he acknowledged his debt to the band, in particular for their theatrical quality and the importance of several strong characters to create dramatic tension on stage. According to Average: 'Kevin Rowland told us he saw Deaf School as this thing which gave him permission to do what he subsequently did.'

'I never realised until recently how much Kevin Rowland was influenced by Deaf School,' adds Enrico. 'I mean, I knew he'd nicked my moustache... It was a big deal for him when he first saw us. After the Magnet gig we had a drink with him and he was telling Vanessa, "I was so influenced by these guys, I even took Steve's moustache and I made the keyboard player have it as well." He actually told me about a whole brass part he'd taken off a Deaf School record for Dexys Midnight Runners. And then of course he got Clive to produce them, the same as Madness did. Those people realised that there was a band here they could relate to. That was inspiring: "I get this. I can do this."'

Clive, meanwhile, came away from the Magnet thinking, 'We've got the feel for it. What are we going to do next?' The answer came a year later, with the opening of another Liverpool venue, the New Picket. The 'old' Picket had been – almost inevitably – situated in Hardman Street and since the 1980s had nurtured the city's musical talent, from the La's to the Coral. Despite support from well-placed friends like Pete Townshend and Elvis Costello, the venue faced closure in 2004, due to property redevelopment. But its founder Philip Hayes fought to relocate, and thus the Picket found its new home in a former dockland warehouse area that is now reviving as the Baltic Triangle.

The Picket's re-launch show, on 27 May 2006, was another milestone evening for the band and for the city. In the audience, Sandra Harris met her ex-husband Roy Holt. Once again, every surviving Eric's veteran seemed to be in attendance, alongside a new generation of Deaf School fans. 'Remarkable,' says Enrico. 'That was the first time I felt like, There's no time in between the band before and this band now.' The momentum was not lost, with more and bigger shows taking place over the next few years. In September 2009 came three triumphant nights at the Everyman Theatre. Max Ripple reflects, 'I think I said at the Everyman to the audience, and it's a kind of a cliché, but "We are Deaf School. You are Deaf School. All together we are Deaf School."'

But the most poignant sight was that of Sam Davis, by now looking frail and only performing with the aid of his oxygen cylinder on stage. The next day, 20 September, they played an outdoor show at the Hope Street Feast. Here, in the shadow of the art college where it all began, was Eric Shark's last appearance.

* * *

Sam Davis died of his lung disease on 7 January 2010, aged 59.

Clive Langer, perhaps, felt closer to Sam than the others did. He'd felt no qualms about being on stage with a frontman who was hooked up to a machine to draw breath. On a purely theatrical level he saw shades of Ian Dury (who was not, in fact, the only disabled player in Kilburn & the High Roads) and Dennis Hopper's macabre prop in *Blue Velvet*.

Sam was special to me, especially in his last few years when we knew he wasn't well. Sam was important. He did the songs that Steve wouldn't sing because they weren't glamorous enough. Without Sam we wouldn't have got 'Knock Knock Knocking', 'Capaldi's', 'Hi Jo Hi'. With me and Steve it's difficult at times, he's a bit off on his own thing: 'I can't do that, it's shit.' Whereas Sam would understand that actually, no, this could be a bit more cool. If you check out the songs I wrote with Sam, they're the cool ones. Steve's songs are a bit of an onslaught; Sam's voice was easier to listen to, in a way. Not a better voice, but more friendly.

He was a laid-back character, he was happy, he let Steve do it. Who was the old English poet, who wrote about love being the line between your eyes? [John Donne's 'The Good-Morrow': 'My face in thine eye, thine in mine appears, And true plain hearts do in the faces rest.'] Onstage, Sam and I would know what was going on. If the sax solo was too long or Steve's talking to the audience too long and it's losing it a bit, Sam and I would be in touch. And that's why I said at his funeral, I just felt whenever I saw him that I was in touch with him. Sam and I, we had a kind of love.

Deaf School was important to Eric Shark, as his widow Joan affirms:

Oh, absolutely. Deaf School transformed his life. He adored the other members of the band. He was less egotistical. He was very much loved by them. He had a lot of *sang-froid*, he was pretty cool and came over as that on the stage. He wasn't one to have hissy fits, or be dramatic or a diva. He was the stabilising influence in a sense, and even in the songs he's a counterpoint to Bette and Enrico. He loved the Deaf School experience.

Deaf School's revival was fabulous, such a tremendous groundswell of fans that re-emerged, and he absolutely loved that. He had a brilliant few years, even though he was really ill towards the end. Again he played that role of the quiet, stable man in the background. He was very sad when Tim Whittaker died. Sam did miss him.

Steve Lindsey noticed the close bond between Deaf School's now-departed comrades: 'Sam and Tim were good mates. They hung out together. They roomed together. They'd sit on the minibus together, get stoned together. Thick as thieves.

We weren't musicians at that stage, though we ended up as musicians to one degree or other. I don't think Tim or Sam felt they were up to scratch. I think there was some insecurity there and they bolstered each other. Sam wasn't a singer in the same way that Steve is, though a great lyricist. He had that air about him of being very calm and cool. I suppose if anyone was like a father figure in the band it was

Sam. Tim was very shy and because they had each other in the band it made it more enjoyable for them. Tim and I would bicker about musical stuff, about the tempo drifting, speeding up and slowing down. And Clive would defend him, because Tim's drumming had so much character. Just minor tiffs. But I never had a cross word with Sam.

The Deaf School website devotes a whole section to people's memories of Sam Davis. Average, once again, pays tribute: 'He was as solid as a rock. He was warm. He was a laugh. He was clever. He was cooler than Coke. I always looked up to him but he never looked down to me. At the heart of the band from day one, he'll continue to be in our hearts.'

ELEVEN

In Town Tonight!

The Catalyst Band – Enrico & Bette xx
– Broken Glass in our Shoes

We are all such creatures of habit
We just can't help sticking around
A little more frayed at the edges
We may seem a little unsound
But still, let the dog see the rabbit
And after the sun has gone down
We'll squeeze out another performance
For the craic, for the roar of the crowd

And let us not fear the reaper
Let's take that imposter to town
And get him blind drunk at the old Pier Head
And onto a ship outward bound!

Enrico Cadillac Jnr, 2013

A troupe of players, well into middle age, had found new audiences for their work. Coping with the deaths of core members, the survivors regrouped and discovered that their pleasure in playing together was undiminished.

The fallen comrades were not forgotten. In spring 2010 the band played memorial shows for Sam in Liverpool and London, the 'Shark Trek' gigs, two of them at the Everyman. 'The deaths in the band were devastating,' admits Clive. 'Tim was so young and we were so young. Sam we never thought would die, he'd just carry on. And Roy, I met him a couple of years ago and he was lovely. He told me he wasn't scared of dying, and I almost made up with him that I'd kicked him out the band. It's not a nice thing to do to anyone, but he didn't hold any grudges.'

More happily, reunion shows since 2011 have featured Paul Pilnick, their guitarist from *2nd Honeymoon* days, still adding that rock'n'roll firepower. We miss those members who have joined the Choir Invisible, but the modern shows do justice to their spirit. No matter that everyone else is older, a latterday Deaf School show celebrates past and present. It honours collective memories, celebrates survival and promises good times yet in store. There is an exhilaration in there: it's the freedom of knowing the future no longer weighs upon you, with all its expectations of career advancement or hip approval.

Still, belated recognition is always nice. A *Guardian* article of 2011 cited Deaf School as one of the ultimate 'Catalyst Bands', the sort that 'toils away in obscurity, loved by a bare handful of fans, that splits without ever being noticed, or whose career just sputters out; then, often years later, their name crops up again and again, cited as an influence by scores of young bands.'

In 2010 Deaf School made their first new record in over thirty years, a mini-album called *Enrico & Bette xx*. It was the first opportunity I ever had to review a Deaf School release and I took advantage in *The Word* magazine:

The Art School Dance Goes On Forever, declared an old album title, and here is new evidence. Deaf School were pure art college, somewhere in the lineage of the Bonzo Dog Band and Ian Dury's Kilburn & the High Roads. They last made a record in 1978, but jubilant reunion shows have indicated something indestructible about the band. So now, 33 years later, they've made a mini-album of new material that picks up exactly where they left off.

Wonderfully, it sounds as fresh and gutsy as the original model. Deaf School are the stopped clock that is right twice a lifetime...

... Part of their supposed problem in the punk days was that Deaf School wanted to be entertainers. Even so, right now I enjoy their wildly contrived 1976 debut, *2nd Honeymoon*, more than nearly anything by the more 'honest' acts of that time. At live shows they are sometimes joined on stage by Kevin Rowland of Dexys or by Suggs, who both know the value of showmanship. There are only five songs on this new collection, but every one of them has a vivid story to tell you. Then the melodies clutch your arm like a madman's bony hand.

Clive Langer, who co-wrote 'Shipbuilding' with Elvis Costello, is once again composing with Enrico (alias Steve Allen) his writing partner. Their bassist Mr Average (alias Steve Lindsey) also contributes, shoring up the classic teen-pop tendencies that

Deaf School always showed when they were not playing at Noël Coward or Marlene Dietrich. There is adolescent nostalgia, perhaps, in the album's title, *Enrico & Bette xx*. And a track that deals directly with that subject, 'The Enrico Song', offers a genuinely touching memoir of one boy's first forays into town at night (*'Mum... Mum. Where's me shirt?'*). The School's saxophonist Ian Ritchie is a stirring presence here, just as he was the first time round.

Bette Bright, whose career after Deaf School also produced some real delights, shines in 'I Know, I Know', a chance to re-visit her affinity for vintage soul-girls like the Marvelettes or Sugar Pie DeSanto. The Suggs connection is brought to mind by another track, 'Scary Girlfriend', with its very Madness-like combination of bittersweet comedy, pub piano and music hall chorus.

So where are we now? The young Deaf School were signed to Warners by the Beatles' pressman Derek Taylor, who honestly believed they were the greatest thing since his other famous clients the Byrds. That, with hindsight, was a fond excess of zeal. And the economics of the music industry have changed drastically since those champagne days. But who knows? This is a fine record. With a puff of breath from some celestial cherubs' cheeks, there may yet be a following wind for Deaf School. And the Art School Dance might go on to delight us a little longer.

Dedicated to Sam Davis, *Enrico & Bette xx* was put together with help from friends old and new. Ian Broudie adds guitar. The drummer is a young man called Nicholas Millard and Clive's producer, later famous for his work with Alt-J, is another rising star, Charlie Andrews. The sleeve design is by Kevin Ward. The inner photo is by Nev Astley. Make-up is by Bette's daughter Scarlett McPherson. There is the strong sense of a cooperative at work.

But Deaf School's experienced old hands know better than most how the economics of the music industry have changed since this band was first on the market. In those days 'getting signed' was everything. Now, you see what you can do for yourself. Maybe you press up your own records, you do gigs – above all, you do gigs – and sell your wares from a table at the back. Mini-album or not, no one should feel short-changed. Clive Langer speaks of it with a pragmatic pride: 'We've got to aim for things that are as special as we can make it. For that EP, we blagged everything. In the end it cost about £4000, and we got strings on it, everything. A Madness record would have cost 50 grand to do five tracks to that standard. I can pull favours in the music world.'

Clive says 'EP'. Enrico prefers 'mini-album':

It's 25 minutes, which by the way is about the same as our second album, I think that was 26 minutes. People were calling it an EP and I'm saying, 'This is enough.' This is where we are in the world of releasing records, MP3s or streaming or downloads, it's what it is. If we have to give it a title it's a mini-album. But basically it's what we can do right now. What do we need? Ten? That old-fashioned idea? No, it's as many great tracks with no fillers as you can get.

I've always written stuff, Clive's always writing, he never stops. I came up with a few ideas. Ken Dodd is in 'The Enrico Song' ['Where's me shirt?'], with a lot of Liverpool references. Hardman Street. There's *In Town Tonight*, which was a show on TV, before the London Palladium, and me mum and dad wouldn't miss that one, and that was the way they announced it, 'In Town Tonight!'

Along the way, a minor but persistent tension in Deaf School was perhaps put right at last. 'What was wonderful, doing that recording,' says the Reverend Max, 'was to see Clive and Ian, who have always been at opposite ends. Ian is a virtuoso who's played with all sorts of people, he believes in the technicalities and he's excellent at what he does. And similarly Clive has a kind of horror of doing things the proper way, the book way. So there was a bit of headbanging. And as a result of this, each suddenly respected the other's position hugely.'

Even Enrico found an improved working relationship with his co-founder: 'It's taken a long time, I had to have a lot of hits with Warner Brothers, as an A&R guy, for Clive to recognise me as someone with an opinion. Before that I'd have let him get on with it. I'm not a producer. But I can sit in on the session and say, This song isn't very good, that chorus could be better. I can do that A&R thing.'

* * *

With an actual new album to promote, Deaf School started performing with a regularity they couldn't have imagined a few years before. Without the need or the desire to suffer the grind of touring, they could select the events that pleased them. And in February 2011, they finally extended their reach to the eastern hemisphere, playing two shows in Japan.

'It's not a massive fan-base,' concedes Ian Ritchie, 'but we have one. The first night was sold out and the second one wasn't, but once we'd done the first night the second one sold out immediately. So clearly that's a building thing. If we went back we'd get double the number of people that were there on the first night and it would grow. I remember this from the '70s: with other bands I played with, people would go "Yeah that's very nice, we'll maybe see you in a year or so," with Deaf School it was always, "When can you come back? Next week?"'

Average describes himself as 'blown away by the whole experience. The Japanese as a people are so well-mannered, you're working hard on stage and sweating, but it's just a polite tapping of hands, no jumping about. Then at the end of the gig you just sense they're enjoyed it. And after the gig we sat down at a long table to sign albums and T-shirts and despite the orderly queue that would form the organisers would practically beat them back into line if they stepped out. Lovely people, earnest and genuine.'

Their former tutor and colleague David Saunders, now living and painting in the south of France, had lost track of Deaf School somewhere after that fabled *Melody Maker* night in London. But even from the Pyrenees he caught wind of Deaf School's second life: 'I was really surprised. I mentioned them to a friend here who hadn't heard of Deaf School, he looked up the Wikipedia entry and when I read it I was amazed. I thought everyone had gone their separate ways. This is not the mainstream yet there is this huge following. What was it that kept the collective together so that it was able to do all these gigs and make all these songs? Something kept bringing them back together.'

In June the band played two closing shows for the Everyman Theatre, due for demolition before being rebuilt. Veterans of Liverpool bohemia sighed for the former Hope Hall and supped their last pints in the downstairs Bistro, a cradle of the city's pop culture to rival the Cavern. In Max's absence (he was teaching abroad), Nick Millard's girlfriend Anna deputised on keyboards and accordion. At the Port Eliot Festival the next month, both she and Max appeared together ('the biggest band we've had for a while,' noted Clive). And in August, Clive, Enrico and Bette played a charity show in Devon with a scratch band called Roxy Mad School, combining them with Suggs and Roxy Music's Andy Mackay, Phil Manzanera and Paul Thompson.

Sandra Harris, the one-time Bright Sister, still goes to see the band when she can: 'Now, if I take someone who's never seen or heard of Deaf School they come away loving it, because there's still that energy. Clive hasn't changed a bit.'

In October they popped up again at the Chelsea Arts Club for Mike Evans' 70th birthday. The room, by sheer coincidence, was still hung with works from a recent Adrian Henri exhibition; looking on were Roger McGough and Holly Johnson. Evans himself was taken by surprise, the more so when his wife smuggled his sax into the building and he found himself leading the band through 'It Should Have Been Me'. 'I knew Deaf School when they could still hear,' he announced.

'I wonder,' Enrico says, 'if Deaf School had made it bigger, what would we be doing now? Would we still be able to do those special gigs? And we have our hits, records that feel like, surely they were hits? They're hits with Deaf School fans. They'll pick out the hits for you, no problem. We still take risks. We like to put a little bit of broken glass in our shoes. I always say, one live performance is worth ten rehearsals.'

And those events will often start, as in days of yore, with Ken Testi collecting the band. 'He loves the music biz and we don't,' says Clive. 'But I really enjoy it when he comes into town. I know this is it: "We're off, get the van." Me and him will load the gear, I'll drive round with him and really enjoy it. It's a bit perverse, like old men being young kids... We'd always take the piss out of Ken cos we'd be driving through London and he'd say, "Hang on, man, I've just got to pop in and see Freddie." Freddie who? "From Queen!" Oh Queen, we hate Queen. We all love them now. I think Ken used to hang around Kensington Market with velvet loons.

'But he's been great, because he's just helped us and never demanded anything. And he's better with money than I am. We need someone to help with the organisation, and he's put his heart into it.'

That 'thread of affinity', as Steve Lindsey described it, seems to run throughout the Dead School collective, where relationships have mellowed over the decades into a relaxed friendship. Bette Bright: 'The thing about Deaf School is that it's actually quite a nice bunch of people involved. We were just like-minded. He's fab, old Steve, isn't he? I do like him. Even though he could be a nightmare to go out with.' Enrico Cadillac: 'It was a bit volatile with me and Anne. Imagine it, two singers in a band. But we're still really good friends. You can see it on the sleeve of that mini-album. There's a lot of affection in that sleeve.'

Bette: 'I never really found it awkward to be the only girl. I would say on the whole they're a pretty nice bunch of people to hang around with. You can sit with them and there'll be interesting conversations going on. Whereas with Madness they'll be squabbling, and you think, *Groundhog Day*. No, I never found that, ever. Everyone's attitude is right. Clive is such a fabulous person. I did once slap him because he was annoying, in Japan, but I've never really had an argument with Clive in all those years.'

Enrico again:

> Deaf School is Clive's life. I never realised how important it was for him, but it's everything. Of all the things he's done, he'd drop everything to do a Deaf School gig. He was the one who wanted it more than anyone else. The truth is that he'd be the first in the rehearsal rooms, the one to organise a get-together. He really wants to be first on stage, but he was also the last to look at the audience when he was on stage. This is the anomaly of it. It's taken me years of pushing Clive forward. I did it on the recent gigs: 'Clive Langer!' and I give him a huge space. Sometimes I have to say to him, Get your arse over there! Because I want people to appreciate him. Clive always looked like this hidden guy, the reticent one. But he was the driving force.

'We all made our own careers,' says the driving force himself. 'We're not lazy people. Everyone's been busy in their lives. And they kept their heads in a very respectable space. There's nothing terrible. There are skirmishes. One of the most outrageous things happened about a year ago, and that was only a slap between members of the band. And Steve did throw a bottle at me once after a gig, but it hit the ground, not me. So that's it. We're not good at being violent. But our dressing room is buzzing and people are taking the piss and chucking things around and then we go on. It's colourful.

'I feel like a very dull person at times, but with Deaf School I feel like a very colourful person. The story has unfolded really well. I started Deaf School and I'm very proud. I stamped myself all over it. I found out I could be a leader. And here we are, still doing it. And the creative spark is not dead.' Enrico: 'We call him Sir Cliff now, like Cliff Richard. That's his new name. Which I think is right, actually. It's not a joke. We feel about him in that way. I mean, he wrote "Shipbuilding", you know?'

Clive says of Max Ripple: 'He's a world of his own, amazing. I don't understand a word he says. No one does. *He* knows what he's saying, maybe it's just too radical. His brain just works in a world of its own. But it's a fascinating, fun world, full of jokes and love of life, love of people. He is actually what the concept at the Deaf School was all about, that Portsmouth Sinfonia thing, looking good and just being a character. Him being on stage is more interesting than some groovy rock'n'roller. There's bits missing of all of us, and maybe when we get together we can fill the gap. We need each other to become this potent force.'

Max: 'Clive had to make some tough decisions, but those are leader decisions and I think everyone respected that. He's a gentle guy but he was never afraid to make a decision. People didn't always agree, but I don't remember there being bad feeling. I think when you get multi-megabucks flying around, that precipitates all sorts of stuff. But we didn't have the privilege of being tested in that way...'

***

Ah yes. Money. 'We never made any money out of Deaf School at any time, really,' admits Clive. 'Creatively, the great thing is that we're still here. I just wish some funeral parlour in America would use "What a Way to End it All" for their ads. But they haven't. And "Taxi" – taxi companies around the world, please listen!'

Enrico: 'We had wages. We had a salary. We're all successful. There was so much talent in that band. There were no losers. No one was afraid of success. You got that in a lot of Liverpool and regional bands, a huge fear of success. I think it's a happy story. We've never had to bale anyone out financially. I did pretty OK. Though I'm nowhere near as rich as those executives in the record label.'

By an irony that's not lost on them, Deaf School developed from anti-musicians, admirers of the Portsmouth Sinfonia, to road-seasoned pros. Max remembers Ken Testi coming to one of the earliest rehearsals: 'And his observation was very illuminating. I thought we'd played this song quite well and he was laughing and said, "That's fantastic, it's just so *loose*." Loose? I hadn't a clue what he meant. It took us years to get to the point where people said, "That's *tight*."'

'Once we really started gigging,' reflects Bette, 'then you had to get better. And Scouse people would go, "Oh you were much better in the old days when it was all ramshackle." But we couldn't go on being ramshackle. I never think I'm a good singer. I can sing all right, but I don't take myself that seriously. Being in Deaf School I was Bette Bright, I wasn't me. I was this "person", this other thing. People see someone like Suggs and he is obviously a recognisable face, but there is more to him, he can be crusty and quite a different persona. I sort of created a character.'

'With other groups,' says Ian Ritchie, 'the success of the performance often has a direct relationship to how well the band play. But with Deaf School there is no connection.

> The band can play really dreadfully but go down a storm, because there's something else going on. Deaf School are by no means the best musical band I've ever played with, but they're the most potent live band. There's something else that got us through. It set us apart from everything else. I've played to 80,000 people at a time, and you've got a stadium filled with people who are there to see that particular artist. But Deaf School were able to do it with people that didn't like us.

Clive Langer: 'We were always trying to write "Friday on My Mind" or "Eloise", we wanted the pop B-movie epics. And I'm still aiming for that. The big epics, "MacArthur Park", let's go for it. "Wichita Lineman", I want to write that. There's a power in Deaf School, there's a power that happens. And where it's going nobody knows. The main thing is, I'm still in love with it.'

Epilogue: Deaf School and the Icelandic Constitution

'**H**AVE YOU EVER READ the original Icelandic constitution?' asks the Reverend Max Ripple. He enquires as casually as anyone else might ask if you watched *Coronation Street* last night.

This will surely be what Ken Testi means when he remembers driving Deaf School around and being amazed by their conversation. It wasn't the standard mix of sexual boasts, money grumbles and competitive farting that you grow to expect on a rock band minibus.

The Icelandic Constitution? I confess it's been a while. Remind me.

'Well,' our man of the cloth continues, 'it's about 8,000 years old. And it starts off something like, "You will lose your hair, you will lose your teeth, you will lose your eyesight, you will lose your house." And so it goes on. "And in the end you will have your reputation."

'Which is a hell of a basis for what's real. A lot of people over the years have this idea when you mention Deaf School that it's still around. People don't always notice when things evaporate; in their minds it's still going. The myth is more powerful than actual experience.'

The Reverend is of course correct. Whether or not Deaf School are currently together in any physical way, their reputation is mighty. The band's existence seems somehow perpetual. In between their several reunions there was even a musical about them, at the 1998 Brighton Festival. There is now talk of another Deaf School musical. Whether or not any band members are actually involved, the sheer *idea* of Deaf School finds a way to manifest itself. It's a strange phenomenon.

If Deaf School were so special, why were they not world-famous? It's a question the band still ask themselves. There is a thirty-five-year post-mortem in progress. Yet things are probably better the way they are. There were no overdoses, no celebrity meltdowns or million-dollar lawsuits. They are not overshadowed by their younger selves, doomed to be half-recognised in supermarkets. They were each free to move on with their lives and did so with great success.

Rob Dickins, who became the Sex Pistols' publisher, remembers their manager Malcolm McLaren coming into his office:

And there was *2nd Honeymoon* at the front of my stack of records. He said: 'They were a great band.' I said I know. And he said something which I've quoted to other musicians ever since: 'But it's just as bad being too early as being too late.' I've seen that so many times. That's the epitaph to me of Deaf School. By the time Johnny Rotten was there with

'God Save the Queen', punk stopped it happening. The planets lined up too late for Deaf School. And two years later they could have kept the name and had the airplay.

Max Ripple puts his finger on a great 'What if?' in Deaf School's history. They came along a couple of years too early for the age of pop videos. What if '2nd Honeymoon' or 'Taxi' had been re-cast as movies-in-miniature for heavy rotation on MTV?

So OK, we got it wrong commercially, but maybe the technology wasn't around, the genres of presentation weren't there. I felt that we'd anticipated the Village People, not because of the gay thing but in the idea that you could put together very different people and make something out of it. A unified whole. I was always a bit embarrassed by what I saw as the soft side of Deaf School, the fact that they didn't seem to have any politics. It seemed like drawing-room amusement. But actually, in some ways it's founded on a sense of an emancipated world.

As Derek Taylor taught me to remember, quality is what matters, not quantity. Deaf School's record sales are of no consequence. It's the romance of their story that appeals to me, and the songs we still have and all the shows that I won't forget. They made a wonderful bid for stardom which did not succeed in its own day, but who cares? They were Cavaliers at a moment when Roundheads were wanted. They were entertainers, in one of those times when pop pretends that it's not show business. As Rob Dickins puts it: 'For a failed band, they were very special.'

Liverpool is where this story began and, although the

story is not really over, it's where we'll leave it for now. From the Cathedral tower we can see the old art school, nicely scrubbed and ready for its next inhabitants. A couple of blocks away, traffic is rumbling past the flats where the School for the Deaf used to stand. Nobody remembers it. We can just make out some distant men of middle years, lighting up outside the Cracke, the Belvedere, the Phil. Are they still arguing about trouser widths? Perhaps they're debating long hair versus short hair, while wishing they had any hair at all.

Down the hill there's a big wheel on the waterfront, by a vast arena and modern hotels, apartment blocks and glossy offices. Still, on some windy corner a red-nosed, cloth-capped man with frost-bitten hands is shouting 'Echo!' Beyond the city's fringes and up the Wirral's spine are the overspill estates. Back in the day, it was all Deaf School's domain. Richard Branson's red Virgin trains flash intermittently between the tunnels from Lime Street station, snake round to Runcorn and disappear to London.

Deaf School were not a Liverpool band and none of them live there now. They were mostly outsiders, drawn to the city in various ways. But they were welcomed. This was an adventurous place with an open mind. The local love for entertainment, glamour and laughter, served up with unstoppable tunes, perfectly matched what Deaf School had to offer. There was a mingling of the sexy with the clownish, of cool satire and frank sentimentality. I hope that my city, led by the better angels of its nature, will not forget to be generous, and will offer a home to many more Deaf Schools in the future.

I once wrote, somewhere, that in the history of the city's music, Deaf School's importance is second only to the Beatles. The quote comes around a lot, not least in Deaf School's publicity material, and I wonder if I was getting carried away. But on reflection, I still believe it to be true.

This book is a fan's gift of gratitude. In a personal way, Deaf School represent the time before I wrote about music for a living, or toiled as an editor at the whitewashed coal-face of the music industry. They belong for me to an age of innocence rather than experience. And that gives them mystique. I have interviewed Madonna at the Ritz Hotel in Paris, but was more star-struck meeting Bette Bright in Camden Town. I have broken bread with Jon Bon Jovi, bonded over Budweisers with Bruce Springsteen and hob-nobbed in presidential suites with U2. But nothing beats an email from Clive Langer or Steve Allen, proposing a curry in Kings Cross next Tuesday.

I'll be there.

Appendix
LIVERPOEM... FIVE 'TIL NINE

Being some versification
By T. JOHN WHITTAKER.
Xmas 1992

PART ONE

What I like about Liverpool is
walking up Park Road 4am.
hearing lark singing,
mid-February thinking
of Spring.

Seeing a ghost see a ghost,
see Chaplin seeing Kerouac,
seeing Dickens see Jung,
see Lennon, Brando and Presley
from a Paradise Street pub get flung.

I like the Old Hall Street
rain,
the soft Saturday afternoon
special summer holiday edition
weather and traffic information
rain.

I like Vauxhall Road's winter razor wind,
all the Granby Street Wunderkind,
going away and coming back
on the next
train.

The city is a Radio.
The city is an Echo.

The city is red sun on red brick
on yellow days,
the City is black rain on black rock on blue nights.
The City is a magnolia tree
in Sefton Park,
and Chinatown Neonlites just after dark.
The city is a woman on Bold Street and you want to
hold her breath.
The city is oceanirishmersey air
she's there again and you stare
to see her standing there,
sorry to digress
but you should have seen her in that dress.

I like the light on the Mersey
from Beresford Road,
light on the Mersey
at Otterspool,

light at the top of the hill
and light at the bottom
by the School.

(Quote: – 'Liverpool and Venice have a relationship
in their shared wondrous quality of Light and Water.'
G. Melly, 1973.)

Later on,
on my bike,
on the way to the Library
and I'm thinking about
George Melly
lecturing at Hope Street in 1973
when I was a different me.
What was it now... something
about Liverpool and Venice
and a geographical quirk
of the light.
making both places
particularly atmospheric
even at night.
The factor of water is involved
I reflect
But my reverie is dissolved,
When on my nose
a spot of rain
I detect.
From this daydreaming I must
refrain, this isn't the Piazza San Marco,
Even if the effect of watery light is the
	same as behind Tesco.

I'll get my head together
and disregard this wet weather.
Well, at least I'm on my bike
and saving shoe leather
or at least I was until later,
much later actually, much
later, in fact, that night.
I went out walking
just after, or just before,
twilight.

When I came back from walking
I couldn't stop talking
to myself and, of course,
my Pet Fish who helps one
to feel less alone
not, mind you, that I
necessarily wish to be
on my own but –
now it's my object
to change the subject
– oh look, it's approaching
the Dawn Zone
hasn't the time flown
I'd no idea.
I'll go to the noveltyagents
and get manipulated
by some media.

Outside I see neighbour's
dog stalking,
I said, 'Boy, for what are
you waiting.'

He said (drumroll) 'The Bone.'
I said, 'Don't do so much talking,
do what you should do
which is mating.
Boy said 'If dog eats dog, soon
only one dog will be left,
of mates bereft,
a final Fido, a last Lassie,
an ex Rex, a canine alone,
the only bone... his own.'
I said 'Boy, your doggerel is vital
but what is the title?'
He said, ' It's called The Dog the Man
was Seen About.'
I said 'Just call it The End.'
Boy said 'Rover and Out.'

Of course, it was still raining
but using my Special Artist
Service training
I got over to the shop
but was ready to drop.
Wet floor, dripping brollys,
wet schoolkids
sucking lollys,
saying yummy,
girls fronts on
fronts of magazines,
girls seem to say come
to mummy.
I say 'The Daily Take please, and
a Tin of Beans.'
I like Mr. Ali and Wife

who are always
quite chummy.

Returning to abode
neighbour seeing me says
'You're up early.'
I said 'No, I'm up late.'
He said, 'Come in, have a cuppa.'
'Thanks a lot mate,
thanks mate,' I said
'but after my supper
it's breakfast and then bed.'
'Okay' neighbour said 'I'll see
you later. Or in your case, soon.'
I said 'Yes, I'll get up
with the moon
or maybe rise
tonight at noon.'
Neighbour said, 'You've stolen that line.'
I said 'Of course it's not mine
but so have a couple of others,
what the heck, we're all brothers.'

I must go to Venice one day
but first the washing-up
I'll get put away.
Then Billy comes round
saying 'What's happening'
I say 'Everything. All the time.'
Bill said 'Oh you're doing another rhyme'
I said 'Well spotted, now Bye Bye Billy
it's well past the Dawn Zone
going on would be silly

in bed I should be laying prone
perchance to dream
Of Merseygondoliers
and for this, Billy,
I need to be alone'
Bill said 'Alright, Greta,
I'll see you later.'
I said 'Right Bill, cheers,
give my love to your Mater.'
He said 'She hasn't been feeling too good.'
I said 'Get her a tonic for her blood.'
He said 'I've tried that
but I think she's allergic to Our Cat.'
I said 'It could be just one
of medicine's riddles,
or failing that try
getting rid of Tiddles.'
'I wouldn't' said Billy 'be all
that fussy about getting rid
Of Mater's pussy
but for that the Old Girl wouldn't stand
even though yesterday it bit her hand.'
I asked 'Was it the hand that feeds it?'
He said 'Yes.'
I said 'Well who needs it?'
He said 'Not me and yet
it's sometimes nice to have a pet.'
'Yes' I said 'and when Horace is fed
I'm definitely off to bed.'
Bill said 'He's a lovely goldfish.'
I said 'Isn't he just,
and he doesn't eat much

just the occasional crust.'
Bill said 'He's asleep, I trust.'
'Yes, he's gone to sleep' I said,
'It looks to me' Bill said,
'like the little chap's dead.'
I shouted 'Horace' and
he started swimming about.
Horace said 'Bye Bye Bill,
close the door on your way out.'
Bill said 'Jings!'
(alluding to his annual Highland flings)
'that fish can speak.'
I shouted 'Billy, go,
before I knock you
into the middle of next week.'

The door slammed but through
the letterbox Billy started to speak
saying 'Sorry Horace,
I didn't mean to shock you.'
I just pretended to be asleep
my temper so as to keep.
Billy called 'I'll see you in a bit,
I've got to take the Kids to school.'
Then without thinking I called
out 'Billy, just what is it
you like about Liverpool?'
Door opened, Bill came back in
so I decided to get up.
I said, 'Some tea I'd be making
but of some things I'm lacking
like, for instance,
another cup.

'I'll have it' Bill said 'in a bottle,
what's that you're reading? Oh,
Aristotle,
I prefer' he said 'Sven Hassel.'
'I like him too' I said
'but not just before bed.'
Bill said, 'I'll come round after,
When I've got the Kids from school.'
I said 'Yes, and then (squeals of laughter)
tell me what you like about Liverpool.'
Billy said 'You'll be just getting up.'
I said 'Yes and bring another cup.'
'Right' Bill said,
'and I'll bring some milk.'
'Okay' I said 'now I'm off to bed
to read some Plato and Rilke.'
'Carpe diem,
William' I said.

END OF PART ONE

PART TWO

... well, about a minute had passed
and I thought great
peace at last
even if a little late
or in my case
soon.

Then guess who came back
through the door,
squelching towards me
across the floor.

Out of his mouth emerged
a large balloon
inside of which was written,
 'It's Pissing Down!'
Bill said 'D'ya like it?
I'm pretending to be a Cartoon!'
A smile of course replaced my frown,
'Like it, Billy?' I said, 'I love it.
You're a bloody clown
but I can dig it.
Now look, Billy, you've got me
in a muddle,
I thought we'd already said
our adieus
and why are you taking off
your shoes?'
Bill said, 'I stepped in a
Liverpuddle
while getting the Kids from school
from where, you said, after
I should come to tell you
(squeals of laughter)
What I Like About Liverpool.'
I said, 'But Billy, you've only been
gone a minute'
'No, T. John' he said. 'Now it's T-time.'
I said, 'Time certainly does Fugit,
I must have been enjoying myself,
I must End my Merseyrhyme
and the book I'm writing
I soon must finish it.
Bill, pass my Taperecorder

off the shelf
oh no, put it back,
nine enormous batteries I lack.
I certainly don't feel like I've
been sleeping,
I must be disentoriated with these horus
I'm keeping.'
Bill said 'What are you calling
this book you haven't finished yet?'
I said, 'It's provisionally entitled
The Fifth Quartet
and what all day
have you been doing?'
Bill said 'Oh, you know... Staying Alive...
... oh, and I did the I-Ching
and got Hexagram Sixty Five.
Look, T. John, there's something
on my mind
and although you haven't much
in the way of good looks
I know you've read
loads of good books
so I'd like your help,
if you don't mind.'
I said 'Maybe in my Hunk Account
there is a deficit,
but what are looks when you can quote in Sanskrit?'
Bill said 'Nothing,
but what if the lady's
deaf as well as blind?'
I said 'Well at least I'm very fit,
I always run the Mersey Marathon'

Bill said 'Well you've got Good Legs,
T. John,
but look, my problem, I need
to share it.'
I said 'It'll help if I write it
down while you recite it,
pass me my pen, turn on the light
but don't go fast
it's very slowly I write'
Bill said 'I'll tell you what I like
about Liverpool first.'
I said 'That is the information
for which I thirst.'
Bill said 'Okay' and started to recite:
'What I Like About Liverpool
is
waiting for a person and
arranging a meeting on
Monday for Tuesday at Three
and you meet on Wednesday at Four
and it's all on for Thursday at Five
when you arrange Friday at Six
which becomes Saturday at Seven
when who should show but she
who sells seashells on the seashore
and she's soon Letting Her Hair Down
all the way to the Dance Floor
where the Beat wears the Crown.'
I said 'Bill repeat that but go slower
I didn't manage to get it all down.'
Bill said 'But T. John, I can't remember
it. I was doing what you taught

me last week about turning my
stream of Consciousness into a river
and using thoughts
as boats.'
I said 'I can't write that fast,
it's just no good,
the rain has turned your river
into a flood.
Were your boats ferrys,
or gondoliers?
It could tell us much
about your inner fears.'
I said 'I need to turn my pen
into a rocket
on the space of this page
and this thoughtship of yours
we need to dock it.'
Bill said 'My train of thoughts
has left the station.'
I said, 'Is it everything you've
forgot
about your previous recitation?'
Bill said 'Under that question mark
you left out the dot,
what you need is a Wodr Prosecser,
Kev'll get you one
for about a tenner.'
I said 'Well for now this pen
will have to do
but this black pen's run out,
Pass me the blue.'
Then again on his tale

Billy set sail,
he said 'I had a pizza once
but it made me sick,
Italian wine my head it makes thick
but I like spaghetti,
that always does the trick.'
I said 'Slow down, Bill,
my hand's not that quick.'
'It's a pity' Bill said 'that Liverpool
hasn't got a plain
where mainly would stay the rain
like the one they have in Spain'
I said 'Repeat what just came out
of your brain.'
He said 'You mean, what I just
said then?'
I said 'Yes.'
He said 'Can't. I've forgotten again.'
I said 'We're not having much success,
I'll have to get some batteries
to record your provincial reveries.'
Bill said 'Provençal's in France
and my memory is bad but at least
I can dance.'
I said 'For that we'll need your video'
Bill said 'I sold it to Kevin ages ago
and provincialism is when an idea
in Idaho is worth not an iota
in Iowa, or even Ottowa.'
I said 'Damn, I missed that as well,
I wish I could write faster, bloody hell!'
I said 'Let's get back to your problem,

sharing 'em usually helps solve 'em.'
Bill said 'Well like I say, you've
read all the books.'
'It's easy' I said
'when you're On Your Tod
and don't spend much time in bed.'
Bill said 'It's not so much a problem
as a question,
what I want to know is, T. John,
do animals believe in God?'
I said 'Do you mean can a
fish be bad?'
He said 'Yes, can a beetle be sad?'
I said 'Can an elephant hate?'
He said 'Do zebras on Sundays
get up late?'
I said 'Is it possible that rodents
experience magic moments?'
He said 'Does a cat love its brother?'
I said 'Does a dog love its mother?'
He said 'Do angry lions count to ten
before they roar again?'
I said 'Do the frog and the newt
discuss the Absolute?'
He said 'Do birds only sing
from nine 'til five?'
I said 'Does work stop for lunch
in busy bees hive?'
He said 'Do geese not take care
of business from five 'til nine?'
I said 'Do horses say that's not
Yours, it's mine?'

He said 'At Xmas, do pheasants
give each other presents?'
I said 'Does a worm in the earth
celebrate its day of birth?'
He said 'Well, what do you think?'
I said 'In deep water, we're about
to sink,
is the Albert open?
Let's go for a drink.'
He said 'It's not usually open
after midnight.'
I said 'Blimey, again Time has
taken a Flight'
Bill said 'It's alright,
I know a late night place.'
I asked 'Does it do a late late breakfast'
He said 'It hasn't in the past
but they might like your face
even though you ain't good looking.
The girl who does the cooking
is called Doreen
and she's a real queen,
by the way, what does
Carpe Diem mean?'
I said 'It's something Horace said.'
Bill said 'Chirpy little chap your
fish, isn't he?'
I said 'No, my fish was named
after the Horace who was quite big
in Ancient Philosophy.
I was indulging in some
verbal horseplay,

(not that you'd notice)
and Carpe Diem means
Seize the Day.
It's something I've been pondering
during my late night wandering,
well... that and one other thing.'
Bill said 'Ah yes, your illustrations
For the I-Ching.'
I said 'Innovations are being made
all the time,
but no, I've been wondering
how to end this rhyme.'
Bill said 'Ask me if there's
anything I don't like about
Liverpool?'
'Alright' I said 'Tell me what
you Don't like about Liverpool.'
'Only one thing' said Bill
'and that's Liverpool City Council.
what about you T. John?
Is there anything about the Pool
that you're not too keen on?'
I said 'There is one thing that
makes me ill'
Bill said 'What's that?'
I said 'Same as you, Bill'
He said 'You mean – '
I said ' – yes, Liverpool City Council.'
Bill said 'Ah, well, you should
end your verse
on a high note,
better not to think of the worse.'

'Or' I said 'best not think
of the worst,
maybe another walk' and I
reached for my coat.
Bill said 'Remember what you told
me in our talk,
about writing down what you
think of first.'
I said 'Yes Bill, I think you're right,
but remember how slowly I write.'
Bill said 'Let me help you again,
It is alright, I brought my own pen,'
and he wrote
 KARP DAYUM
and we strode off into the night.
Then Horace spoke
to get the Last Line
'What a lovely bloke,'
he said in his fishy whine.
'Don't go changing,
William.'

But I return in black,
Horace said 'Oh, you're back.'
I said 'It doesn't matter what's the day,
it's the way you seize 'em.'
Horace said 'What a thrill...
but the Last Line must go
(even though he karn't spell
... oh, what the hell)
to
Bill.

Dec 25 1992

UK Discography

1. Original Albums

2nd Honeymoon
What a Way to End it All; Where's the Weekend?;
Cocktails at 8; Bigger Splash; Knock Knock Knocking;
2nd Honeymoon; Get Set Ready Go; Nearly Moonlit
Night Motel; Room Service; Hi Jo Hi; Snapshots;
Final Act
(Warner Bros vinyl and cassette, 1976)

Don't Stop the World
Don't Stop the World; What a Jerk; Darling; Everything
for the Dancer; Capaldi's Café; Hypertension Yeah Yeah
Yeah; It's a Boy's World; Rock Ferry; Taxi; Operator
(Warner Bros vinyl and cassette, 1977)

English Boys/Working Girls
Working Girls; Golden Showers; Thunder and Lightning;
What a Week; Refugee; Ronny Zamora; English Boys

With Guns; All Queued Up; I Wanna Be Your Boy;
Morning After; Fire; O Blow
(Warner Bros vinyl and cassette, 1978)

2nd Coming
What a Way to End it All; Shake Some Action; Hi Jo
Hi; Nearly Moonlit Night Motel; Taxi; Ronny Zamora;
Thunder And Lightning; Blue Velvet; Princess Princess;
I Wanna Be Your Boy; Lines; Capaldi's Café; 2nd
Honeymoon; Final Act
(Demon vinyl and CD, 1988)

Enrico & Bette xx
U Turn Away; The Enrico Song; I Know I Know;
Goodbye to All That; Scary Girlfriend
(Deaf School CD, 2011)

2. Compilations and Reissues

What a Way to End it All: The Anthology
What a Way to End it All; Where's the Weekend?;
Cocktails at 8; Bigger Splash; Knock Knock Knocking;
2nd Honeymoon; Get Set Ready Go; Nearly Moonlit
Night Motel; Room Service; Hi Jo Hi; Snapshots; Final
Act; Don't Stop the World; What a Jerk; Darling;
Everything for the Dancer; Capaldi's Café; Hypertension
Yeah Yeah Yeah; It's a Boy's World; Rock Ferry; Taxi;
Operator; Last Night; Working Girls; Golden Showers;
Thunder and Lightning; What a Week; Refugee; Ronny
Zamora; English Boys With Guns; All Queued Up; I
Wanna Be Your Boy; Morning After; Fire, O Blow

Plus the following BBC John Peel sessions:
What a Way to End it All; Where's the Weekend?;

Knock Knock Knocking; Final Act; It's a Boy's World;
Capaldi's Café; What a Jerk; Hypertension Yeah Yeah
Yeah; Working Girls; All Queued Up; English Boys With
Guns; Ronny Zamora
(Castle CD, 2003)

2nd Honeymoon
As per vinyl/cassette version, plus Ding Dong; Waiting
for You and the following BBC sessions: What a Way
to End it All; Where's the Weekend; Knock Knock
Knocking; Final Act
(Lemon CD, 2009)

Don't Stop the World
As per vinyl/cassette version, plus Love on the Wire;
Goodbye to All That and the following BBC sessions:
It's a Boy's World; Capaldi's Café; What a Jerk;
Hypertension Yeah Yeah Yeah
(Lemon CD, 2009)

English Boys/Working Girls
As per vinyl/cassette version, plus Dustbin Sweetheart;
It Should Have Been Me and the following BBC
sessions: Working Girls; All Queued Up; English Boys
With Guns; Ronny Zamora
(Lemon CD, 2009)

3. Singles

What a Way to End it All c/w Nearly Moonlit Night
Motel
(Warner Bros, September 1976)

Taxi c/w Last Night
(Warner Bros, January 1977)

Thunder and Lightning c/w Working Girls
(Warner Bros, February 1978)

The Survivor Song c/w Knock Knock Knocking (live);
Capaldi's Café (live)
(Deaf School, March 2010)

Sources

Books and Articles

Adams, Roy, *Hard Nights: My Life in Liverpool Clubland* (Cavernman, 2003)

Biggs, Bryan, 'The Art School Dance Goes on Forever', unpublished paper for Tate Liverpool symposium, *The Art School Dance: Art into Pop, Pop into Art*, 2007

Bowen, Phil, *A Gallery to Play to: The Story of the Mersey Poets* (Liverpool University Press, 2008)

Bracewell, Michael, *Re-Make/Re-Model: Becoming "Roxy Music"* (Faber and Faber, 2007)

Cornelius, John, *Liverpool 8* (Liverpool University Press, 2001)

Du Noyer, Paul, *Liverpool: Wondrous Place* (Virgin, 2002)

Edwards, Terry, *One Step Beyond* (Continuum, 2009)

Fallows, Colin, 'Keynote Essay', unpublished paper for Tate Liverpool symposium, *The Art School Dance: Art into Pop, Pop into Art*, 2007

Florek, Jaki, and Paul Whelan, *Liverpool Eric's* (Feedback, 2009)

Frith, Simon, and Howard Horne, *Art into Pop* (Methuen, 1987)

Hardstaff, Steve, *Cover Versions* (Liverpool University Press, 2008)

Hignett, Sean, *A Picture to Hang on the Wall* (Michael Joseph, 1966)

Johnson, Holly, *A Bone In My Flute* (Century, 1994)

Keoghan, Jim, 'Eric's Was King', *Record Collector*, April 2012

Madden, Paul Terence, *Madden's Liverpool* (Madden's Guides, 2012)

Pih, Darren, 'Liverpool's Left Bank', in Christoph Grunenberg and Robert Knifton (eds), *Centre of the Creative Universe: Liverpool and the Avant-Garde* (Liverpool University Press and Tate Liverpool, 2007)

Schwartze, Klaus, *The Scouse Phenomenon* (Druckerei & Verlag Bitsch, 1987)

Sharples, Joseph, *Liverpool* (Pevsner Architectural Guides, 2004)

Simpson, Dave, 'Catalyst Bands: What Do You Mean, You've Never Heard of Them?', *Guardian*, 21 July 2011

Strachan, Robert, 'Liverpool's 1970s Bohemia', in Marion Leonard and Robert Strachan (eds), *The Beat Goes On* (Liverpool University Press, 2010)

Sykes, Bill, *Sit Down! Listen To This! The Roger Eagle Story* (Empire, 2012)

Thomson, Graeme, *Complicated Shadows: The Life and Music of Elvis Costello* (Canongate, 2004)

Warner, Simon, 'Raising the Consciousness? Re-visiting Allen Ginsberg's Liverpool Trip in 1965', in Christoph Grunenberg and Robert Knifton (eds), *Centre of the Creative Universe: Liverpool and the Avant-Garde* (Liverpool University Press and Tate Liverpool, 2007)

Willett, John *Art in a City* (Methuen, 1967; republished with new introduction, Liverpool University Press and the Bluecoat, 2007)

Websites and Periodicals

deafschoolmusic.com
ian-ritchie.com
langerwinstanley.com
Liverpool Echo & Daily Post
Melody Maker
NME
Record Collector
Sodajerker.com podcast with Clive Langer and Steve Allen, by Simon Barber and Brian O'Connor, August 2012
Sounds
The Word

Index

Letters in italics refer to pages in the plates section